A Search for
What Makes Sense

Finding Faith

Zondervan Books by Brian D. McLaren

Brian D. McLaren
Foreword by Steve Chalke

A Search for
What Makes Sense

Finding Faith

ZONDERVAN®

ZONDERVAN.com/
AUTHORTRACKER
follow your favorite authors

Finding Faith — A Search for What Makes Sense
Copyright © 1999, 2007 by Brian D. McLaren

Previously published as parts 1-2 of *Finding Faith:
A Self-Discovery Guide for Your Spiritual Quest*

Requests for information should be addressed to:

Zondervan, *Grand Rapids, Michigan 49530*

Library of Congress Cataloging-in-Publication Data

McLaren, Brian D., 1956 –
  Finding faith : a search for what makes sense / Brian D. McLaren.
    p. cm.
  Includes bibliographical references.
  ISBN -10: 0-310- 27266-1 (softcover)
  ISBN -13: 978-0-310-27266-3 (softcover)
  1. Apologetics. 2. Faith. I. Title.
BT1103.M35 2006
202 – dc22   2006034754

Interior design by Michelle Espinoza

Printed in the United States of America

06 07 08 09 10 11 12 • 20 19 18 17 16 15 14 13 12 11 10 9 8 7 6 5 4 3 2 1

This book is dedicated to all who are seeking faith, spirituality, purpose, hope, and God. The fact that you care enough to seek means that you have already found more than you may know.

Contents

Foreword

The Brothers Karamazov, the great novel by Fyodor Dostoyevsky, is the story of three brothers torn apart by guilt after the murder of their father. In the best-known chapter, atheist intellectual Ivan tells his younger brother, Alyosha, about a dream he had. In it Jesus returns to earth in the sixteenth century, during the time of the infamous Spanish Inquisition, to the city of Seville.

Appearing with no fanfare, Jesus travels on foot to Seville Cathedral and promptly finds himself being arrested by the ninety-year-old Cardinal Grand Inquisitor. The Inquisitor visits Jesus in prison, calmly telling him he will be burnt at the stake the next day. Jesus says nothing as the old man details the charge against him. He'll be killed, the Inquisitor explains, because he jeopardizes people's salvation. He gives them too much freedom. People may all have been born with freedom, the Inquisitor goes on, but it's only a tiny elite who actually have the moral strength and courage to cope with it; who possess the ability to believe in the face of uncertainty; to have faith when all around are in doubt. The majority of folk just aren't up to the demands of the task.

"I tell you," the Grand Inquisitor continues, "humans are pathetic creatures, with no more urgent need than to find someone to whom they can surrender the gift of freedom they were born with." This, he explains, is what Jesus failed to understand the first time around. By refusing to give in to his temptations in the wilderness or come down from the cross — actions that would have proved his power and identity beyond all doubt — he saddled the peoples of the world with the crippling burden of uncertainty. "We've corrected your mighty achievement," the old man boasts, defending the brutal way in which the Inquisition forced people to believe the church's doctrines. "They'll accept whatever we tell them with joy, because they'll have been spared the anguish and torment of having to make their own, free, and independent choices."

One thing that the old Inquisitor was right about in his assessment was Jesus' consistent refusal to do things that would force people into believing in him. Instead, he always allowed room for doubt and presented people with the opportunity to explore their questions. He never pushed, forced, bludgeoned, beat, coerced, cajoled, manhandled, or manipulated people into faith — he never threatened them with "an offer they couldn't refuse." In contrast to the high-handed "interventionist" approach some who follow Christ have adopted, his efforts to bring the people he encountered into a closer relationship with God were characterized by the slow, steady undertow of grace. He had what we often lack — the maturity to see that faith isn't something you either have or don't have, but something that ebbs and flows in the life and soul of every individual. Doubt isn't the opposite of faith. It is an element of faith. Where there is absolute certainty, there can be no room for faith.

Jesus never compelled people to believe. Instead he *invited* people to have faith. And that's very different. He accepted that even his closest and most loyal followers (the church's future leaders) would have their doubts and their misunderstandings. Rather than demanding absolute certainty or doctrinal orthodoxy from his followers and adopting a policy of "zero tolerance," he encouraged them to explore their doubts, ask their questions, and express themselves honestly.

Many people crave certainty. They don't want to have to think, agonize, or grapple with life's difficult questions for themselves. Instead they want dogma. They want guaranteed answers. They want shoot-from-the-hip certainty. This book is not for them. Rather, Brian McLaren's work is for those who want to think, who want to bring their doubts and questions, struggles and problems with faith for an honest conversation. "Instead of trying to tell you what to believe or focusing on why you should believe," he writes, "my goal is to help you discover how to believe — how to search for and find a faith that is real, honest, good, enriching, and yours." Later he adds, "I won't pretend to have no beliefs myself — that would be dishonest. Instead, I'll try to be open about my own conclusions without imposing them on you."

"A perfect faith is nowhere to be found," French Reformer John Calvin once explained, "so it follows that all of us are partly unbelievers." One could wish that all of his followers shared this same opinion. A few years ago I read an account in a national newspaper by a man who, after years of unhappiness, had left the church and abandoned his faith. In the article he explained why he had taken this difficult step. He chose to finish his piece with a short conclusion that has stayed with me ever since. It simply read: "I'm happier to live with questions I cannot answer than to live with questions I cannot ask."

I would like to think that this gentleman will somehow have the opportunity to read a copy of this book — I have a sneaky feeling it might just help to restore his faith.

Steve Chalke, MBE
Founder of Oasis Global, Faithworks,
and www.Church.co.uk

Preface: A Note to My Readers

Several months ago I took a day off to walk along a favorite stretch of the Potomac River, where it winds through the Appalachian Mountains before entering the coastal plain of Maryland where I live. It was a day to think, to sort through some of my questions and doubts, to struggle with some new understandings that were forcing my faith to adapt and stretch to new dimensions. It was also a day to think about what would go into this book.

I remember reaching a certain point along the old towpath just below one of the locks of the old C & O Canal. A very simple thought dawned on me there: *I need faith.* Here I am, someone who is writing a book on faith, and I am realizing as never before how I need faith, not only to live my daily life to the full, but also to grow and nurture and sustain my faith itself and, too, to write the book you are now holding.

I suspect that the very act of reading this book will be an act of faith for you, just as writing it is for me. Realizing this, I imagine you now walking with me alongside the river and you and I being, as of this moment, on a journey of faith together. This book can become our extended conversation.

I realize that for some readers it is easy to relate to the experience of walking along a beautiful bend in a river, speaking of faith, shaded by tulip poplars, sycamores, and black, white, and red oaks. Many readers have friends with whom they can easily and freely share their questions about life and its meaning and purpose, their stories of faith and doubt, their struggles with deep questions that murmur in the back of their minds like the river beside the path.

But I know that other readers find it hard to relate. Perhaps you have nobody you can talk to about these matters; your faith journey is, so far, a lonely one. Or perhaps the whole subject of faith is painful for you. For you, faith is make-believe, self-hypnosis, manipulation, group hysteria, anti-intellectualism, obscurantism, closed-mindedness, backwardness, guilt, pressure, dishonesty — these negative images or associations clash harshly with the image of a peaceful walk along the river. Or maybe for you, faith is like death or sex, a subject you know you shouldn't deny or avoid, but one that is profoundly uncomfortable. You wish, and I wish for you, that faith could be a subject of joy, vitality, hope, and healing.

It is for people like you — people who struggle with faith — that I have written this book. The people for whom faith comes easily and whose faith is never called into question probably would never pick up a book like this anyway (although I wonder if it might do them some good if they did).

I am grateful for the people of Cedar Ridge Community Church in Spencerville, Maryland, who have helped me learn faith in so many ways (www.crcc.org). A community of faith where love and hope abound is a too-rare thing these days, and such a community of faith that provides a safe place for people who express questions and doubts is even rarer. I am privileged to enjoy such a community.

Both in the church and in my associations outside of it, I have made many friends who would call themselves atheists or agnostics, or who follow religious paths very different from my own. Several of them (Glenn, Gregg, Tony, and others) agreed to read this manuscript and "field test" it for me. I thank them for their insights, questions, and responses, which have made this a better book than it would have been.

As always, I am grateful for my best friend and partner, Grace, and for our four amazing kids, Rachel, Brett, Trevor, and Jodi, who are launching their own journeys of faith. Of course, I could also mention the one to whom I am grateful for all of these wonderful people, and for the beauty of that stretch of the Potomac River, and for all of the rich experiences of life. But that's getting ahead of myself, because that's who this book is ultimately about.

Let's keep walking together.

Introduction:
Why Is the Search
for Faith So Hard?

I think I reached my first faith crisis at about age twelve. From my earliest childhood, I have loved science — especially learning about animals and nature. (I will still choose a nature show on TV over just about anything else.) By the time I finished junior high school, I had checked out and read almost every nature-related book in our local public library, including a couple of college textbooks. My first faith crisis hit when someone at my church said that people had to choose between God and science. I just couldn't understand this.

Looking back over the subsequent years, I would say that "crisis management" described my faith experience. It was a cyclical story of hope followed by disillusionment, elation at finding "the answer" or the ultimate faith formula followed by depression when the easy answers and formulas didn't work. At several junctures I imagined that I would live the rest of my life without faith — finding and keeping faith was just too hard.

But somehow, in the process of seeking a faith that is real and makes sense, I ended up with a faith that has sustained me. That faith still involves crises from time to time. It hasn't provided me an exemption from life's ups and downs, nor has it given me a "get out of doubt free" card. But somehow, my faith has evolved from being part of the problem of my life, something I was always trying to resolve, to part of the solution for my life, something that most often sustains me and gives me resources to face life's challenges.

Through all of these experiences of faith, I have never forgotten what it feels like to be in the midst of struggle, when faith is a problem, when finding and keeping faith seems impossibly difficult. I hope my reflections on faith can be of some help to you, whether you are seeking a faith you have never had, trying to recover a faith you lost, or trying to hold onto a faith that seems to be slipping through your fingers.

Dimensions of the Quest

Let's be realistic about the tough challenge you're taking on. This quest is no Sunday school picnic. To begin with, you are going to have to think harder and bigger than you ever have, because although good faith isn't limited to the mind, it requires the mind to be fully engaged.

The search for faith also involves noncognitive parts of us — emotions, longings, aspirations, dreams and hopes and fears, drives, desires, intuitions, and experiences. It often forces us to face some ugliness in ourselves, some hard facts about life and our world, requiring courage, honesty, and determination. Faith involves admitting with humility and boldness that we need to change, to go against the flow, to be different, to shine the harsh light of scrutiny on our cherished illusions and prejudices and face them with candor, and to discover new truths that can be liberating even though they may be difficult for the ego, painful to the pride. The search for a faith that makes sense has been the most challenging and life-changing quest of my life. Nobody should expect something this important to be easy.

Whom Can You Trust?

Another challenge: To whom do you talk about this search? Perhaps you could go to a minister, pastor, rabbi, or priest. But don't they have a vested interest in the outcome of your search? Can you trust them to be unbiased, or might they push you, stack the deck, suppress some evidence and inflate other evidence, trying to sell you on their brand, subtly making it hard for you to say no?

You might go to a counselor, but then again, the counselor may see your search as a pathology and try to cure you of it.

It's not always easy to consult your spouse, either. "Searching for God? I just wish you would help with the dishes or clean out the car," you might hear. Or, "You don't have to become more spiritual, dear, just less grouchy." Or, "So now it's spirituality. I wonder how long this will last." A friend's response might be similarly discouraging: "Oh, great! Does this mean you won't play cards with us anymore? Are you going to make us hold hands in restaurants and pray before we eat? Will I have to apologize from now on if I say a four-letter word in front of you?"

You might consult a college professor of comparative religion or a historian conversant with the development of world religions, someone for whom the subject is purely abstract and academic. But might her very objectivity and professional detachment create another set of problems? Wouldn't you find yourself apologizing for taking this whole thing so seriously — so personally — in the first place? Wouldn't you find it hard to express your personal longings in the company of someone who studies those very personal longings as sociological or psychological or historical phenomena?

Thankfully, there are some friends, ministers, counselors, and professors who could be of real help to you in your search, who understand your desire for unhurried and unpressured guidance, who will not coerce you to conform your search to their expectations, who will offer guidance while leaving room for you to reach your own conclusions. I hope I can be of help to you in precisely this way. I have served as a pastor for twenty-four years, but before entering ministry, I worked in higher education, as an academic counselor and college English instructor. Over the years, I have become more and more sensitive to the predicament of the intelligent adult — young, middle-aged, or senior — who begins searching for faith, for spirituality, and for God. I can't pretend that I am completely neutral, a totally objective third party. Here is my bias: *I sincerely hope you find what you are looking for.* I hope you will become one of a growing movement of people who are seeking "good faith" — the kind of faith that will make your life a better life so you can help make our world a better world. It is toward that end that I am dedicating myself in these pages.

Your Search

If I understand you and your situation correctly, there are two things your search is not. On the one hand, it is not an act of desperation. You are not in such a frenzied or fearful emotional state that you are willing to believe anything as long as it brings relief. Sadly, some people are reduced to this condition, and they jump on the assembly lines of cults and extremist groups, ready to conform, ready to make false confessions, ready to sacrifice their personal responsibility for the benefit of belonging to a group that is sure about everything.

No doubt there are troublesome things from which you seek relief, and conversely, better things you desire: a sense of purpose for your life, perhaps; forgiveness and peace to replace the guilt and fear that nag you; an integrated philosophy or worldview that makes sense of life with all its grandeur and squalor; an explanation for the spiritual experiences and sufferings that have come unbidden into your life. But these triggers to your search require something more than a desperate emotional placebo for you. You would actually aspire to know some truth. Your search is for a relationship with a God who really exists, and if no such God exists, then you want to know that too, straight up.

On the other hand, your search can't be reduced to a merely objective, detached, theoretical, academic investigation. One of my favorite novelists, Walker Percy, loved to picture the difference between your search and the more objective, abstract type of search with a story that went something like this: Imagine a group of physicists and astronomers gathered for a lecture on cosmic background radiation. As the lab-coated lecturer drones on, the scientists are listening, taking notes, rubbing their chins, crossing and uncrossing their legs, maybe nodding a bit, occasionally mumbling, "Interesting," or something of that sort. Suddenly, a woman walks briskly onto the stage and whispers something in the lecturer's ear. He hands her the microphone and she says, "Ladies and gentlemen, a fire has broken out in the lobby. Please stay calm. Leave quietly and quickly through the exits on your left. Do not use the rear exits, as they are already smoke-filled and unsafe. Please follow me — this way."

At this moment, no one keeps rubbing his chin, crossing and uncrossing her legs, taking notes, or mumbling, "Interesting." The reason? Before, during the lecture, their situation allowed them the luxury of abstracted, disinterested detachment. But now, their real-life situation has been addressed, and the category of communication has changed from *knowledge* or *information* (a lecture on astrophysics) to *news* (of a threat to safety and life and how to escape it). Flooded and numbed by information as we are, it is often hard for any message of news to get through to us. Life often has to send us some pretty strong wake-up calls to make us susceptible to news, open to it, hungry for it. You may have had some of those wake-up calls to bring you to this point. Or perhaps it is simply the sense that, as the philosopher Blaise Pascal said, "we are embarked" — the realization that you are on a journey going from somewhere to somewhere for some purpose, and you don't want to finish your journey without exploring its purpose and direction.

So, here you are. You are not just an abstracted listener in a lecture series about the psychology of spirituality, the demographics of religion, the history of theology, or theoretical ethics. Rather, you have had your wake-up call. You are a person who knows you are alive, who feels the immediacy of "something more" in life that has never been adequately accounted for. You are a person who knows you will one day die, and who feels the urgency of finding your place in the universe before you vacate it. You are a person who wishes to be honest and feels dishonest either when denying the existence of a spiritual dimension to life (as some secular people may pressure you to do) or when repeating without question someone else's creed (as the religious folk may pressure you to do).

Three Needs

Many of us were brought up with some sort of faith as children. Our parents, our extended family, our ethnic group, our society likely reinforced their religious views in us. But as we grew older, we questioned many of the beliefs that were passed on to us. Perhaps we saw hypocrisy all too evident in the lives of the religious, or we asked questions our tradition didn't answer. Perhaps we saw religion repeatedly being used to inspire hatred or fear or conformity, and we have grown suspicious or disgusted. Perhaps we have met good people of other faiths and have felt that their goodness somehow makes our faith generic, inferior, or superfluous. Or perhaps we learned things from science, history, or philosophy that contradicted the tenets of our faith, so we rejected our faith or sidelined it for so long we forgot it was there. Perhaps our initial coming into faith was part of our adolescent identity crisis, tied in with youthful idealism ("Let's change the world through God and love and belief!"), alienation ("At last, a group that accepts me!"), insecurity ("Maybe God can help me take a shortcut around the difficulties of growing up."), or even rebellion ("I'll show my parents—I'll change religions!"). Or perhaps we found ourselves "faithfully" going through the motions, but never really feeling or experiencing anything ourselves. Eventually, we could not sustain the charade, or we just lost interest.

One way or another, we outgrew the faith of our childhood or youth. Now we are seeking for a faith that we can hold with adult integrity, clear intelligence, and open-eyed honesty. So, many of us need in this way to renew or replace the faith we lost—to fill the old vacancy in a new way, to see faith with fresh eyes, or better—to let a mature, refreshed faith become the new eyes through which we see life.

Others of us have faith, but it is weak or damaged. We feel that we are walking on a sprained ankle or trying to enjoy a delicious meal with a bad tooth. Perhaps we have been spiritually undernourished, malnourished, or mistreated and injured by a church or religious family member. We don't have confidence in our faith, and it brings us more pain than comfort. Or we have a faith that is little more than a set of concepts to us. This kind of faith is often called nominal, meaning "in name only." It doesn't affect our behavior, at least, not positively. Perhaps for some of us, faith is like a vaccination—we have just enough in our system to keep us from getting "infected" with a full-blown "case" of vibrant faith. There's faith there, but it needs to be "set on fire"; it needs to come alive; we need to really "catch" it. In these ways some of us need to invigorate the faith we already have.

Still others of us were brought up in a secular context. Faith to us seems strange, an oddity, an embarrassment, superstitious, primitive, the customs of "some other family's culture"—natural to them but foreign to us. Yet we find our secular worldview unfulfilling, able to tell us much about the world, but unable to account for much of our own experience as men and women. We need to find the faith we never had before.

That is the purpose of this book: to help you replace the faith you lost, invigorate the faith you have, and develop the faith you desire but never had before.

More "How" Than "What" or "Why"

Like you, I am a spiritual seeker, and I have many friends who are spiritual seekers at varying stages in their journeys. Obviously, my work as a pastor has rooted me in a community of such people every day, so the struggles of spiritual seeking are always on my mind. This is the book that I wish had been there to help me and my friends in our own spiritual searching. I hope it will help you. I hope it will encourage relationships and conversations among spiritual seekers wherever it is read—relationships and dialogue that will be mutually beneficial and encouraging in many ways.

Originally, *Finding Faith* was one book of 300-plus pages. Some readers told us they favored the first half of the book, and others raved about the second. Eventually we decided it would make sense to let each half of the book stand alone, with this first volume focusing on the more intellectual questions and the second on more experiential matters. So in this volume, we will discuss questions like what faith is, how faith and knowledge are related, whether God exists, and how thinking people can explore and evaluate various ideas about God. In the second volume, we will explore questions about how people can experience God, how they can relate to God on a day-to-day basis, and how they can strengthen their faith through spiritual practices such as prayer and solitude and even going to church.

In both books, instead of trying to tell you "the answers" via dogmatic pronouncements (as many well-meaning people have already tried to do for you, no doubt), I would like to try to help you find the answers yourself. Instead of trying to tell you what to believe or focusing on why you should believe, my goal is to help you discover how to believe—how to search for and find a faith that is real, honest, good, enriching, and yours.

My job will be to lead you to and through important questions, in a sensible order, since good questions are among the most important tools for a good journey. While some questions tend to lead to dead ends or vicious circles of controversy, other questions, approached in a sensible order, can help a person progress in his or her search at a good pace, not rushing, but not wasting time either. Rather than presenting one answer only—what I might feel is the "right" answer—I will try to guide you through several possible answers and encourage you to make your own choices. Again, I won't pretend to have no beliefs myself—that would be dishonest. Instead, I will try to be open about my own conclusions without imposing them on you. You may agree with me; you may not. I will feel I have been of some service to you either way simply by stimulating your thinking.

Along with questions, I have found that stories can be of great help in the search, so you will find many true stories—my own and others'—included in each chapter. (As you would expect, I have changed some names and details to avoid invading anyone's privacy.) Most of my own faith story can be found in the companion volume, *Finding Faith—A Search for What Is Real*, for those who would like to continue the conversation beyond this book. But even the intellectual questions that will be the focus of this book grow out of my own story. For me, intellectual matters are intensely personal matters too. One of my main credentials as a pastor is that I myself have had most of the doubts or spiritual problems anyone else has ever come to me with, so I hope the accounts of my struggles in this book and its sequel will offer you something to identify with and learn from too.

Reader-Friendly

There is no one right protocol by which to search for God. There is no simple formula or easy recipe that you can follow to arrive at faith. The way that is most natural for me to express my understanding may not be the way that is most natural for you to progress in your understanding. The physicist and the artist,

the social worker and the engineer, the salesperson and the pro-
grammer will approach the spiritual search differently. That is
why I encourage you—in fact, I urge you—to skip around and
read the chapters first that are most useful for you.

Here is a quick self-assessment that can help you determine
where to start, what to skip, and so forth.

Which of these statements best describes you?

- My problems with faith are primarily philosophical
  and intellectual. (If so, you should start with this
  book, and skim the table of contents for the questions that are most urgent for you.)
- I already have a basic faith in God, but I am eager
  for more spiritual experience. I already have a conceptual kind of faith; I want a faith I can feel. (If so,
  you may wish to skip this book and pick up *Finding
  Faith—A Search for What Is Real* instead.)
- I want to know more about who you are and what
  you believe. (If so, you should begin with chapter 3
  in this book, and the last few chapters of *A Search for
  What Is Real*, which tells a bit more about my own
  experience with faith. You also might want to go
  to my website—brianmclaren.net or check out my
  book *A Generous Orthodoxy* [Zondervan, 2004].)

The chapter previews should also help you determine which
chapters would be the best starting point for you. At the end of
each chapter you will find a section called Your Response, which
can be used in two ways. First, if you write your responses, you
will compose a kind of personal creed, which can serve as a
personal manifesto or record of your spiritual journey. Second,

if you use these questions for dialogue with some friends, you can enjoy one of life's greatest pleasures — people talking openly about life's deepest matters. Following the response section, you will find recommended resources (books, CDs, DVDs, websites, and more) and finally, sample prayers, which can help you express and exercise your faith as it grows.

For the Already-Convinced

If you are already a convinced believer of whatever religious persuasion, I hope you will understand that my real focus here is not to engage people like you. Many other books (including some of mine) aim to do that. My goal here is to help the unconvinced person — the seeker, the questioner, the skeptic, the doubter, the reflective — for whom there aren't enough helpful resources yet. To be of the most help to him or her, I may have to disappoint you. I am sorry about that.

In that light, I hope you will understand why I may not validate some of your most dearly held doctrines, or push for closure and definition as you might, or use terminology that you might prefer. Also, please understand that we live in a very dynamic time, what some people describe as the hinge between modern and postmodern worlds. Many of the answers that were most helpful to people twenty-five years ago land with a thud today, and other questions that we never thought of twenty-five years ago are electric and unavoidable today. As C. S. Lewis said in his introduction to *Mere Christianity*, "You can not even conclude, from my silence on disputed points, either that I think them important or that I think them unimportant. . . . All this is said simply in order to make clear what kind of book I was trying to write."

If you are one of the already-convinced, I hope this book will help you learn ways to be more understanding of and therefore more helpful to your spiritually seeking friends. I hope so, because books take people only so far, and then friends are indispensable. (If you would like to read the story of a friendship that grew from this book, check out *More Ready Than You Realize* [Zondervan, 2002].) In fact, if you are a credible person of faith, your life itself offers more important data for your spiritually seeking friends than anything I could write. The best use of this book will likely be as an extended foreword or footnote to the message of faith that is told through the life you are living. In that way, I am honored to be your colleague.

Together, through your life lived well at close range, and through my words in this book, I hope we can help more and more people find faith. Then more and more lives will begin to reflect the benefits of a healthy spirituality, which will positively affect still more people. The ripples can spread far, so let's get started.

Your Response

1. Here is a brief description of my religious background:
2. Here are the more positive features of my religious background:
3. Here are the more negative features of my religious background:
4. My primary goal in reading this book is to ...

   ... replace the faith I lost.
   ... invigorate the faith I have.
   ... develop the faith I desire but never had before.

Part 1

Faith, Knowledge, and Doubt

Does It Really Matter What I Believe?

This chapter attempts to define faith by distinguishing "good faith" from "bad faith." These important terms will be used throughout the book. It also explores the problem of "circularity" (that arguments about faith often seem to be circular arguments) and the idea of a "leap of faith."

Who Should Read This Chapter?

If you have heard or made the statement, "It doesn't really matter what you believe, as long as you're sincere," this chapter is a must-read for you. This chapter is also for you if you are bothered by the fact that faith seems to make many adherents into worse people, not better people.

What Questions Does It Address?

What is faith? What is bad faith? What is good faith? How can I "get into" faith if I feel like an outsider?

Overview/Diagram

A General Definition of Faith

Bad Faith   Good Faith   Circularity and the Leap
                                        (or Step) of Faith

The most beautiful and profound emotion we can experience is the sensation of the mystical. It is the source of all true science.... To know that what is impenetrable to us really exists ... this knowledge, this feeling, is the center of true religion.

Albert Einstein

Does It **Really** Matter **What** I **Believe**?

I t doesn't matter what you believe, as long as you're sincere." That must be one of the most common statements I hear when people first start talking about faith. What do you think about that statement? Personally, I don't think these people really mean what they are saying, at least not literally.

- They couldn't mean that it's okay for a crazed cult leader to sincerely believe his sincere followers should join him in sincerely drinking poisoned Kool-Aid so they can end up in heaven together sooner rather than later.
- They couldn't mean it's okay for white supremacists or anti-Semites to believe and practice their beliefs, as long as they are sincere — which, I say with sadness and disgust, they often seem to be.
- They couldn't mean it's okay for totalitarian dictators to suppress religious freedom, since they are sincere in believing religion is an opiate of the masses or a menace to their regime.
- They couldn't mean that it would be okay for sincere religious fundamentalists to control the lives of millions through sincere intimidation, censorship, legislation, or threats of violence.

- They couldn't mean that it would be fine with them for parents who believe that life is meaningless to raise their children with a nihilistic philosophy of life, freely offering their children drugs, for example, or allowing them to experiment with vandalism and violence, not caring about their education or motivation, abandoning any pretense of teaching moral guidelines, since they sincerely believe that nothing really matters.

The kinds of people who I have heard talk this way about sincerity would never agree with these implications of their statement taken literally.

Nor would these people want to be associated with the abandonment of truth that their statement seems to imply. They would never mean to invite people to the disaster of sincerely believing dangerous illusions. An analogy to walking on ice can help here. If you are walking on a lake that's covered with one inch of ice, no matter how sincere you are in believing you can do it, you are in for a cold soaking at best. If someone encourages you to try, "as long as you're sincere," they are no friend!

(Conversely, if you are walking on a lake that's covered with twelve inches of solid ice, even if you are plagued by doubt at every step, you will still be upheld. Of course, if your doubts are so great that you never get out on the lake at all, you will never know either way.)

So, the issue is less the sincerity or intensity of your faith than it is the trustworthiness of the object of your faith: Is it solid enough, deep enough, trustworthy enough, to be capable of holding your weight? From this vantage point, the "as long as you're sincere" statement seems hard to justify, I think you will agree.

But in a more positive light, when people say, "It doesn't really matter what you believe, as long as you're sincere," I think they are trying to make an important distinction we will explore (and endorse, I hope) in this chapter: the distinction between "good faith" and "bad faith." The Latin term *bona fide* means, literally, "good faith"—and I think we all sense that some examples of faith ring with an authenticity, a sincerity, and a quality that qualify them as "bona fide" faith, good faith. Conversely, some examples of faith strike us as inauthentic, unwise, unsubstantial, "bad faith." The "it doesn't really matter what you believe" statement, in this light, means, "As long as you have a good faith—a faith that enriches your life, makes you a better person than you'd be without it, and doesn't cause harm to others—I don't want to quibble about details."

If that is the case, I think people who make this statement realize something quite profound: "Right faith that isn't good faith isn't really right faith." (Faith that believes true things but does so in an ugly or inappropriate way is not justified just because it is conceptually correct.) They might even be going further: "I would rather have a wrong faith that is good than a right faith that is bad." (I would rather hold some inaccurate beliefs with a good heart, so to speak, than be accurate in all the details and yet have the wrong approach, the wrong attitude.)

What do you think about those statements? It seems to me that people with good faith will by definition want to keep learning, humbly acknowledging the truth whenever they discover that some of their beliefs were imbalanced or inaccurate or incomplete. They will regularly fine-tune and adjust their beliefs to be more in line with what they are learning. If that is true, wouldn't people with good faith come, over time, to have an increasingly accurate faith? In other words, isn't the goal of a right faith best served by concentrating hard on a good faith? If that is the case, how should we define good faith? Even more basic, how would we define faith?

A Provisional Definition of Faith

Maybe you heard about the little boy in Sunday school who defined faith as "believing what you know ain't true." We have to do better than that in our definition of faith. Let's start like this: *Faith is a dynamic state of relative certainty about matters of ultimate concern sufficient to promote action.*

Let me forewarn you: We are going to come back later and quarrel with this definition a bit. We will challenge it, expand it, and improve it. But for now, let's use it as a springboard and break it down as follows:

1. Faith is a *state*. Faith is a condition we find ourselves more or less "in"—like being in good health, or in love, or in depression, or in ecstasy, or in confusion, or in doubt. I suppose that psychologists could study it as a psychological phenomenon, perhaps finding certain electrochemical patterns in the brain associated with faith. But faith is also more than a condition or feeling. It is more than just something we experience. Faith is the context in which we feel and experience and think about everything in life. It includes data—propositions, ideas, specific beliefs—that form an intellectual framework, a paradigm, in which all other psychological phenomena take place and by which they are evaluated.

A crude analogy to a computer might be helpful. The operating system of the computer is the "state" in which the computer operates. It provides the foundation and framework upon and within which all the operations of the computer occur. Faith is, in this analogy, the operating system of the computer. It is the state or condition or system a person operates in. But that is not to say it is "static," though. As we will see, good faith continually self-modifies, like an operating system that continually upgrades. In this sense, faith is a *dynamic* state.

2. Faith is a state of *relative certainty*. As we will see in the next chapter, we humans don't seem to have the luxury of absolute, unquestioned certainty in many (if any) areas of life—and especially in matters of the spiritual life. So we acknowledge our predicament—that we have to function in relative certainty, which always includes relative uncertainty.

3. Faith is a state of relative certainty *about matters of ultimate concern*. We are not talking about abstract mathematical equations or the middle name of the vice president or the cost of green beans at the grocery store. We are talking about how we conduct our lives, make our decisions, solve our moral dilemmas, face death and the possibility of afterlife for ourselves and other people, cope with suffering and loss, answer the big questions about our origin and destiny and ultimate value, decide whether life is worth living, establish values, and so on.

Matters of ultimate concern are matters of truth. In this light, good faith can be distinguished from pretending, self-hypnosis, self-delusion, manipulation, or lying by its intention to reach for truth, reality, what's there. In other words, faith is an attempt to orient oneself to and concern oneself with what is real and true both "in here" (subjectively) and "out there" (objectively). Some thinkers have used this expression: True faith is held "with universal intent." Believing is thus distinguished from make-believe in that the person "in" faith believes she is onto what is actually universally true, not just what is "nice" for her to fantasize about to make herself feel better. She hopes that she is not departing from reality, but rather closing in on it, through her exercise of faith. To proceed otherwise would be to act in "bad faith."

4. Faith is a state of relative certainty about matters of ultimate concern *sufficient to promote action*. How much certainty is sufficient to qualify as faith? If a professed belief is not sufficient to promote action, then it would be better called an opinion or an idea or concept. We may hold it as data in our memory banks, but it does not constitute part of our operating system. If an idea (say, that God exists) doesn't promote action (say, to search for God or pray or monitor one's own moral behavior or love one's neighbor), it isn't really faith at all ... it's just an idea. But if we are so committed to an idea that we act on it, then it ceases to be a mere idea. If we are so committed that we take action—action as simple as reading a book like this, attending a church service, admitting a fault, reaching out to an estranged associate, showing compassion to a person in need, or reaching across a barrier of fear or prejudice—there is real faith at work.

Given this definition, faith seems like a needed thing, a good thing. Why then would anyone want to reject faith? Again, when people say they are rejecting faith, I don't think we should take them literally. Rather, I think what they really mean is that they are rejecting "bad" faith. They have decided that the operating system they inherited or installed is "no good." It doesn't work for them. Maybe it can't account for the data presented by real life. Maybe it doesn't make its adherents into better people.

Maybe it is too complicated to be useful. Maybe long-term it is too boring or depressing to be livable. For these and other reasons, people often "lose faith," meaning they discard their version of faith. Perhaps this describes your situation, but now you find yourself wondering if you have, to use two clichés in rapid succession, thrown out the baby with the bathwater and jumped from the frying pan into the fire. You wonder if there are more than two alternatives — bad faith or no faith.

Bad Faith Descriptors

1. In my view, bad faith is based solely on unquestioned authority. In other words, in bad faith, I believe simply because an authority figure or structure tells me to. I don't think for myself. I don't question. I comply, thoughtlessly believing what I am told to believe. Maybe I am lucky — maybe I happen to follow the one right authority structure; but what of all those poor folk who blindly follow authority structures that direct them to believe differently? Should they be condemned and I praised simply because I was lucky enough to have blindly followed the right guru, or been born into the right family who happened to belong to the right religious denomination?

Clearly, tested and trusted authority figures, structures, and organizations can be of great help in developing a good faith (in fact, later we will talk about the value of participating in a faith community) — but no responsible adult can blindly, mindlessly follow the group if one wants good faith. Good faith doesn't appear to be a herd behavior. (The dynamic relationship between authority structures and an individual's questioning and commitment is complex and has important implications for parents trying to pass on a good faith to their children. Too much pressure and they threaten to ruin what they are trying to strengthen; too little guidance and they inadvertently imply that the subject just isn't that important.)

2. Bad faith is based on pressure or coercion. At a party I attended a few years back, I asked a woman—a visiting scholar from another continent—about her religious beliefs. Then, perhaps to be polite, or perhaps from genuine curiosity, she asked about mine. We seemed to be having a pleasant, animated conversation about "matters of ultimate concern." After a while though, she became increasingly uncomfortable. "In my country, it is not permitted for me to question my beliefs, and listening to you talk about your beliefs is raising doubts about my own. It would not be permitted for me to convert to another religion or even to become lax in performing the duties of my religion. I would be shunned by my community and disowned by my family. So, I must not continue this conversation."

With that, she walked away. I was stunned, and these thoughts came to mind: This coercive approach may make for national solidarity in her country. It may keep attendance high at religious services. But it doesn't make for an authentic faith sincerely held.

Of course, this characteristic of bad faith is found not just in other countries. Here in America, I have run into many cultic groups with a similar coercive edge. But even beyond cults, we are all largely unaware of the ways the groups and cultures in which we participate pressure us to conform and chastise us when we rattle the cage—of consumerism, rationalism, nationalism, scientism, and so forth. We are so used to the subtle "tyranny of the majority," which often takes hold even in our religious communities, that we seldom buck it. How much of what we believe right now is the result of our buckling to the pressures of the culture we are part of? We may not be so different from the visiting scholar I met at that party after all.

3. Bad faith is often the result of a social or psychological need for belonging. Maybe no one is coercing me to believe, but if I am so desperate to belong that I will claim to believe anything the desired in-group requires of me, how can my faith be authentic? I recently saw this dynamic in a teenager I know. She is a very social person but has always had trouble making friends. Through her high-school years, she has experienced the unbearable adolescent pain of being labeled different or uncool and being excluded from the "in group." She found no acceptance anywhere until she encountered a group of similarly alienated young adults who practice witchcraft. I know she has no idea what they believe or why, but now she calls herself a witch as an expression of her relief at finally being accepted, of finally belonging to some group.

4. Bad faith appeals to self-interest and base motives. I recently heard about missionaries of a certain religion in a certain country who actually pay people to attend their services. I have also heard about religious groups that use sexy young women to allure male members. Less extreme, but no less inauthentic, are those groups that promise health or wealth, revenge or power, pain avoidance or easy solutions to all life's problems. This approach violates the "matters of ultimate concern" element of our definition. I doubt God would be very impressed with those who believe in order to become rich, popular, comfortable, lazy, and so forth, with no real desire for the true, the good, or the beautiful.

5. Bad faith is arrogant and unteachable. When a person takes pride in feeling "right" and rewards himself with a sense of superiority, when his faith puts him in a high and mighty posture to look down in judgment on others, it's hard to feel that we are dealing with good faith. When religious people indulge in spiritual status-seeking (Look at how much I give! Notice how much I suffer! Aren't you impressed with my knowledge, my piety, my zeal?!), their desire for attention seems even more disgusting than those who parade their material wealth in a quest for social status. That know-it-all spiritual attitude, that pretended certainty that makes one talk, talk, talk but never listen, that obnoxious "you can't teach me anything I don't already know" spirit — these traits are ugly in the irreligious, pathetic in the religious.

6. Bad faith is dishonest. If I boldly proclaim, for example, that the earth is six thousand years old, when I have convincing evidence that it is much older, I may outwardly appear faithful, but don't I lack integrity? If my religion tells me to believe that members of another race or group are inferior, when I know many of these people personally as wonderful people, don't I become a worse person by continuing to recite the "party line"? When I have witnessed corruption in a religious organization firsthand, but continue to publicly uphold it as pure, can I be showing good faith? How could a God of truth be pleased by my saying things I do not mean?

7. Bad faith is apathetic. Since real faith inspires action, if my faith produces no action, it cannot be good faith. If I cannot honestly say that my faith makes a difference — if I would behave just as I do without my faith — then my faith is bad faith or cheap faith, if it is faith at all.

Sometimes this lack of action is covered by a surplus of talk. Sometimes the jargon flows thick, like lots of strawberry jelly on moldy bread. Sometimes people substitute the active life of faith with the fascinating lore of faith — terminology, facts, opinions on religious esoterica, and so forth. This immersion in words no doubt positions these adherents well to win at religious Trivial Pursuit, but that's about it. Who is fooled by the barrage of words, besides the talker himself?

8. Bad faith is a step backward. Perhaps I am a young adult, growing up, just graduating from college. I become frightened by career choices. I seem to be striking out in the "dating game." I am paralyzed by the challenges of adulthood. If in this context, I join a highly authoritarian religious group so that someone else will make my decisions for me, my faith is really an excuse for immaturity. If I am overwhelmed by advances in science, by complexities in ethics, by gray areas in my own personal life, and I throw myself into a religion that tells me easy answers so I don't have to think for myself, my religiosity is an excuse for laziness and fear rather than a motivation for growth and courage. Good faith ought to produce good fruit; I ought to become a better person for holding it. A faith that makes me less loving, mature, wise, alive, or responsible sounds to me like bad faith.

In writing this book, I asked several of my friends (agnostics and atheists) to read the manuscript and give me their feedback, all of which was helpful and some of which was downright profound. As I dialogued with one of my friends, something became clear to me in a whole new way: Healthy people don't step backward or down; they only step forward or up. This insight explains both why some people leave faith and others accept it; in either case, their move into or out of faith is perceived by them as a step up. For this friend, brought up in a rigid, anti-intellectual religious system, science (in this case, science as a package deal with atheism) — honest, accurate, curious, open-eyed — felt like a huge step up from the superstitious version of religion he had been presented with. I would have to agree with him; it was a step up. As we continue our dialogue, I am hoping he can see that the best alternative to "bad faith" in God is not necessarily no faith (or faith in the science-atheism package). Granted, to step back into the version of religion he grew up in would be a step down, but perhaps there is a step that will present itself to him that will be a step up into good faith.

These descriptors of bad faith are my opinions, and you may disagree. But perhaps they will ring true. At the very least, I hope they will stimulate you to develop your own working descriptions. As I will say again later, I don't think the greatest enemy of monotheism is atheism, agnosticism, polytheism, dualism, or pantheism: It is bad monotheism — monotheism carried out in bad faith. Show me a person who has rejected faith, and nine times in ten I will show you a person or group nearby who turned him or her sour with their example of bad faith. That is why I believe that our world is in such desperate need — not of more religion, and not even of more faith — but of more good faith. But what exactly is good faith? Let me tell how I describe it.

Good Faith Descriptors

1. Good faith is humble, teachable, and inquisitive. If I am aware of how contingent and limited my knowledge is, how can I be conceited about how much I know? How can I look down on someone else for knowing less? Isn't conceit — the sense of certainty that I am already so right and superior that I don't

need to learn or listen — the greatest possible barrier to faith? In this way, isn't religious conceit the most hideous sin imaginable because it is incredibly dangerous and ridiculous? If there is a God, wouldn't good faith begin by humbling oneself before God, acknowledging one's ignorance, and asking for guidance and enlightenment?

If I am appropriately humble, isn't it possible that anyone can become my teacher, from a little child to a mental patient, from a sage of old to a comedian of today? Isn't an open mind that is eager to learn the essence of good faith (as it is of good science)? Aren't yesterday's certainties sometimes the enemies of tomorrow's faith, since we will be tempted to say, "The old ways are good enough; I don't need any new approaches"? Shouldn't humble, childlike inquisitiveness be characteristic of good faith, since I am young, new here, with an awful lot to learn? Wouldn't it make sense to ask God my questions and see if any answers are forthcoming?

2. Good faith is grateful. If I reach some conclusions as I humbly and teachably continue on my search, some working hypotheses to base future experiments upon, shouldn't I be grateful for them? Even if they are only a few very basic things, such as "God exists and loves me and wants me to imitate God by loving everything God loves," aren't these few basic things very precious and worth celebrating? Even if I can't claim to comprehend (or grasp completely) everything, can't I acknowledge that I have at least apprehended some things (having at least touched them, come into contact with them, begun to experience them)? And rather than being puffed up by this "knowledge," shouldn't I be grateful to God and others for helping me learn what I have learned, being sure not to close myself off to further learning?

3. Good faith is honest. Shouldn't I feel free to be as accurate as I can about what I am relatively sure about and relatively unsure about? Shouldn't good faith feel free to express both doubt and confidence, neither overstating nor understating its level of certainty? Shouldn't I abhor dishonesty, since it clouds the already difficult search for truth? Shouldn't I seek to honestly acknowledge and remove my own blind spots before critiquing others about theirs? Shouldn't I be as honest about my own weaknesses and those of my community of faith as I would want others to be about theirs?

4. Good faith is communal. Since my individual understanding is so limited, don't I need connection with a group of trusted companions, so we can help and encourage one another in our common search for faith, God, and truth? Don't I especially need friends — a faith community — who will gently confront me when they see me losing these qualities of good faith? And just as I value highly my cohorts in my faith community, don't I also need honest, humble dialogue with people of other groups (religions, ideologies, parties, denominations, and so forth), since they may see things I am missing, and vice versa? And shouldn't humility and teachability prompt me to include in my faith community people from the past, so I can learn from the writings and art of the great sages through history? Granted, we don't want coercion and pressure, but don't we need mutual encouragement and support from other seekers, past and present, in our spiritual search?

5. Good faith is active. If I apprehend what I believe to be truth, am I not obligated to live by it? Shouldn't I abhor apathy (not acting on my beliefs), hypocrisy (covertly acting contrary to my beliefs), and inconsistency (overtly acting contrary to my

beliefs) just as I abhor dishonesty? Shouldn't my pursuit of truth be hot rather than lukewarm—suggesting a hunger and thirst for more truth, rather than complacency about what I believe I have already found? And if I believe the search for truth and faith and God are indeed important, shouldn't I sensitively try to influence others (who are open to my influence because I have earned their respect) to take steps forward in their own search—always without coercion?

6. Good faith is tough. How much is an easy, untested faith worth? If faith brings all benefits and no costs, how can I be sure my belief is an honest pursuit of truth and goodness, as opposed to a pursuit of benefits? If my faith always gains me respect and compliments, and never rejection or misunderstanding, might I not just be a believer out of social convenience? My faith may feel strong today, but how will it fare under tomorrow's tragedy, depression, disappointment, or delay? When money is tight or when money is flowing freely, when friends are few, when temptations are enticing, when patience is thin, when I am in the middle of a project and the end seems to elude me, will I abandon my faith? Is a faith that doesn't cost me anything worth anything? Is a faith any good that doesn't challenge me to do good and become better, even when I don't feel like it?

7. Good faith is relational. If I believe there is a personal God behind (and with) the universe, shouldn't my search for truth in God's universe begin with an acknowledgment of my relationship with God? In other words, given my personal limitations and the limitations of human knowledge, wouldn't it make sense to live in dependence on God to help me learn and search fruitfully—and more, to live with expectancy and hope that God will in some way be my teacher and guide? Wouldn't

my relationship with God thus become the basis or context for my search for truth? And shouldn't I consider what loyalties and responsibilities are incumbent upon me as a party in this relationship with God?

Circularity

You might ask at this point, "But how can I have a relationship with God if I am not sure God even exists?" You might even say, "This is very frustrating. You say I need faith to find a relationship with God, and then you say that having a loyal, trusting relationship with God is a necessary component of good faith. This is very circular and frustrating!"

You raise a good point. Your frustration now will serve to push us beyond the limits of our original working definition of faith (which we said from the start would need some improvement). You may have noticed that our original working definition never even mentioned God; it presented faith as if it were simply an internal reality ("a state of relative certainty," we called it) with no vital connection to anything (or anyone) beyond oneself. In that provisional definition I was trying to avoid this circularity that we must now come to terms with.

Some concepts or theories can be entered into via linear argument, from A to B to C, and so on. But some conceptual frameworks — we could call them worldviews or paradigms — are systems unto themselves, and in that way, they do seem circular from the outside. One can make an approach from the outside. One can observe and assess, evaluate and compare. But the only way to test them from the inside is to jump in (hence the phrase, "leap of faith") and investigate them by experiment and experience. In other words, you can study a car, talk to other drivers, research its specifications, and compare it with other models, but if the indicators are positive, eventually you will want to test drive it, which requires actually getting inside of it.

I think of a bright young graduate student who came to see me last year. He had been raised in a churchgoing family, but in college had lost whatever faith he had. He heard that I was someone who understood the kinds of questions and doubts he struggled with, and he drove for two hours just to talk with me. At the end of our session, he expressed a desire to come back again, and I encouraged him to bring a list of specific questions so that we could be sure to address them directly.

In our second meeting, he pulled out his list and we began to deal with his questions, one at a time: How can evil exist if there is a good and powerful God? Why are there so many religions? Who is to say that some things are morally wrong? Midway through a question about sexuality and morality, he interrupted me: "Just a minute. This isn't what I need at all. Our time is so limited, and I am quite certain that you will have a logical answer for every question I have on this paper." After a pause, he continued. "I don't want to talk about faith from the outside anymore. I want to move to the inside and see the answers from the inside. The answers will come in time. The important thing right now is for me to move from the outside looking in to the inside." Can you identify with this young man? There is a point where enough questions have been asked and answered, and you are ready to take the step, or make the leap, to proceed in your search from within the circle of a faith-relationship to God.

Long Leaps or Short Steps

Be assured, I have no desire to push or rush you in that direction. I am going to do my best to present all the linear, step-by-step logic I can, so that when the time is right, if you choose to make a move from your current circle to a new one, it will be a manageable leap, or maybe even a single short step. That is all that's required, really. In fact, I think you can imagine that first step of good faith as a kind of simple "Hello! Is anyone there?" shouted into the darkness.

The act is absurd, in a way. If no one is there, I am shouting to no one and making a fool of myself. Yet if someone is there, how can I know it if I don't take this risk ... this risk of faith? In order to find if someone is there, I have to act as if I already know that someone is there. The call into the dark is, in that sense, circular, presupposing that someone is there, and more, someone who speaks my language, is predisposed to respond, is friendly, and whose acquaintance and response would be welcome. Significant presuppositions to be sure! But that is our situation with faith. There is a risk involved (the risk of being wrong) and a certain circularity (of needing to believe, however tentatively, certain things about God—such as God's existence and desirability—in order to begin searching for God). I think that this risk and circularity are inescapable. I can't see any way around them. Can you? If I sincerely want to know if someone is "out there," then sincerity will move me to take the risk and make the call out into the darkness.

Still Working on the Definition

I said earlier that our working definition was a start, but not the last word in defining faith. We have since taken a step forward by adding the adjective "good," and we tried to define what we would mean by "good faith." We have acknowledged that logic alone will not get us "into" faith, but we have expressed a desire to make the leap into faith a sane, manageable, reasonable one. But I still think we should admit there is more to faith than we have said so far. Our understanding of faith will have to grow as we proceed, but one thing is, I hope, becoming clear: It really does matter what you believe, and even more, it matters how you believe.

A Quiz

Let's finish this chapter with a two-question quiz. The purpose of the quiz isn't to pass or fail you, but to challenge you to think.

Multiple-Choice Question

If I take my four children on a walk by the river, and we sit together on some rocks and watch the river run by, and in that quiet moment I say to them, "Rachel, Brett, Trevor, Jodi ... I love each of you. I really do. I hope you will believe that"—which of the following seven responses would I be happiest to hear from them, in what order, and why?

A. "Sometimes I doubt that. But I'm open to being persuaded that it's true."

B. "Can you give me a genetic analysis of your DNA and mine so I can have greater certainty that you are indeed my biological father?"

C. "Could you repeat that? I was so engrossed in watching the river that I didn't hear what you said."

D. "In that case, I would like a new car, unlimited use of your credit card, a phone line of my own, and a complete overhaul of our typical diet."

E. "Why then did you give my brother a birthday gift that cost $8.75 more than mine last year? I've been keeping track, you know."

F. "Thanks, Dad. I believe you do. And I love you too."

G. "Yeah, whatever."

True–False Question

T or F: The fact that you are reading this book indicates some degree of good faith, as does the fact that you want to continue reading and thinking. Even your questions, disagreements, and push-backs to what you are reading indicate the presence of good faith.

Your Response

1. I affirm the following descriptors of bad faith:
2. I affirm the following descriptors of good faith:

Resources

The film *The Mission* explores the effects of faith on two men and the agonizing issues they face as they try to apply faith to life. The contrasts between the good faith of these two and the bad faith of the institutional church are staggering and troubling.

Carl Sagan's film *Contact* similarly explores issues of good faith and bad faith—both in religion and science.

Prayer

I do not want to develop a faith that is sincere but misguided. On the other hand, I don't want to develop a faith that is conceptually accurate but heartless or graceless. I want to learn, and as I learn, I want to be increasingly aware of how much more I have to learn.

What Is the Relationship between Faith and Knowledge?

This chapter examines the words "know" and "believe," and argues against the common myth that we human beings have a clear-cut choice between certainty, science, and knowledge on the one hand and faith on the other. It considers, and rejects, the religious claim that the Bible or some other document can provide certainty. It suggests that even science, which we normally think of as being purely rational, has important nonrational elements, and has more in common with faith than most people realize.

Who Should Read This Chapter?

This is one of the more philosophical chapters in the book, and so is especially for folk of a more analytical, reflective bent.

What Questions Does It Address?

How much can we really be certain of? Is some degree of faith inescapable, or is it possible to live without any faith at all? Are religious people justified when they say the Bible gives them certainty?

We have but faith; we cannot know,
for knowledge is of things we see;
And yet we trust it comes from thee,
A beam in darkness; let it grow.
Let knowledge grow from more to more,
But more of reverence in us dwell;
That mind and soul, according well,
May make one music as before,
But vaster.

Alfred, Lord Tennyson, "In Memoriam"

... my not being able to give a sufficient reason is not a
matter of a defectiveness in my ability to think, but of a
real peculiarity in my relationship to the one whom I trust
or to that which I acknowledge to be true. It is a relation-
ship which by its nature does not rest upon "reasons."...
Reasons of course can be urged for it, but they are never
sufficient to account for my faith.... My rationality, my
rational power of thought, is merely a part, a particular
function of my nature; when however I "believe" ... my
entire being is engaged, the totality of my nature enters
into the process, indeed this becomes possible only because
the relationship of faith is a relationship of my entire being.
But personal totality in this sense can only be involved if
the whole function of thought, without being impaired,
enters into it....

Martin Buber, *Two Types of Faith*

2

What Is the Relationship between Faith and Knowledge?

In the preceding chapter I stated rather nonchalantly that good faith was about the pursuit of truth. But in postmodern times, it's dangerous to use the word "truth" naively. As never before, we are sensitive to how hard it is (some would say impossible) to know truth. We are increasingly aware of the ways our presuppositions, politics, and subjectivity color our perception, interpretation, understanding, and communication of "the truth"—and as a result, we aren't at all sure that what we have at the end of the day is even worth calling "truth."

In my opinion, the problem we face is less with the word "truth" than it is with the word "knowledge." Few if any of us doubt there really is something "out there" called truth. But increasing numbers of us are suspicious of humans' ability to perceive, interpret, understand, and communicate what is out there with a degree of certainty worthy of the word "knowledge."

A Thought Exercise

So let's think about the word "know" for a few minutes. Consider these sentences:

1. I know the capital city of Uzbekistan.
2. I know I exist.
3. I know that 4 x 13 = 52.

4. I know that water is two parts hydrogen and one part oxygen.
5. I know Tim Ayers.
6. I know the town of Hancock, Maryland, like the back of my hand.
7. I know a bargain when I see one.
8. I know that black holes exist.
9. I know that Abraham Lincoln was an American president.
10. I know that Abraham Lincoln was a great American president.
11. I know the meaning of the word "flangma."
12. I know God exists.
13. I know God.

What do you make of the various uses of "know" in these statements? In which cases does the word "know" mean complete, unassailable certainty? How many different meanings does the word "know" have in these statements? How do you know? Now consider the word "believe" in these situations:

1. I believe it's going to rain.
2. I believe in extraterrestrials.
3. I believe in liberal democracy.
4. I believe the square root of 9801 is 99.
5. I believe Abraham Lincoln made a mistake in launching the Civil War.
6. I believe I can be a success.
7. I believe that music is a universal language.
8. I believe it because I saw it with my own two eyes.
9. I believe it is safe to swim in that lake.

10. I believe that all mammals bear live young.
11. I believe that God exists.
12. I believe in God.
13. I believe God.

How do these two words, "know" and "believe," relate? How might knowledge and faith relate? It appears that some people can believe just about anything, but how much can people really know?

Knowing about Knowing

The study of certainty is called epistemology. Epistemology gets you thinking about questions and problems related to knowing and believing—problems like these:

1. Have you ever forgotten anything—an appointment, an important birthday, something at the store, where you left your wallet or keys? Have you ever had an automobile accident that was your fault—due to a lapse in attention or judgment? If your mind is capable of having important memory lapses or being responsible for serious accidents, how do you know when you can trust it?

2. Is it possible that you are really insane, so insane that everyone knows it but you? Is it possible that everyone is just humoring you, pretending that you are normal, but you are actually out of touch with reality? Or maybe you are dreaming. Maybe you are a character in someone else's dream, and of course this whole thing seems real, since the other person's imagination wills you to think it's all real. How do you know these possibilities aren't true?

3. The Eskimos, we are told, have dozens of words for snow. They would never think of saying, "It's snowing," any more than

we would say, "It's precipitating," or, "Weather is occurring." The statement is simply too general to be of any use to them. The specificity of their language causes them to see differences among types of frozen crystalline precipitation that the rest of us don't even notice. Is it possible that my language similarly blinds me to many important spiritual distinctions or realities that others who speak different languages may grasp? And is it possible that human language in general guides our thoughts into ruts that keep us from knowing reality in other—perhaps truer or fuller—ways? Is it possible to train our minds to go beyond the normal limits of our languages?

4. In ancient times, everyone "knew" the earth was flat. Before Galileo's day, everyone "knew" the sun revolved around the earth. Before Darwin's day, everyone "knew" the earth was created in six literal days about 4004 BC. Before the Civil War, many people "knew" that slavery was completely justified. How do we know that many of the things we think we know today won't be shown to be false in the future?

5. After the highly publicized O. J. Simpson murder trial in the United States in the mid-1990s, most people of the same race as the accused "knew" he was innocent, while most people of other races "knew" he was guilty. All had heard the same objective evidence, but their subjective interpretation of it was, in some cases at least, influenced by their background. How do we know our backgrounds haven't impaired our ability to be objective or fair?

6. Most people brought up in the context of a particular religion believe that religion is true. If you are born in India, you are probably going to "know" Hinduism is the true religion; if in America or Guatemala, it will probably be Christianity; if in an

intellectual family in France, agnosticism or atheism; if in Iran, Islam; if in Israel, Judaism. There are exceptions, but it appears clear that the majority of people choose their beliefs based on social acceptance, peer pressure, and other factors rather than on a sober independent investigation of the objective evidence. How many of the things we "know" simply reflect the norms of the groups we belong to?

7. Scientific knowledge is based on repeatable experimentation. As data increases, as hypotheses "work" under repeated testing, one makes an inductive leap from specific results to generalizations, which are accepted as "knowledge." Is something true because it works consistently?

Uncertainty Principles

Clearly, the words "believe" and "know" signal a lot of complexity, a lot to think about. It doesn't seem possible to assign some arbitrary "certainty factor"—so that if your certainty is less than, say, ninety-four percent, you "believe," and if it is ninety-five percent or greater, you "know." How would one apply such a number—based on a "gut feeling"? How do you "know" your "gut feeling" is accurate? Someone might suggest that the word "know" be reserved for only 100 percent certainty, but again, one has to question whether 100 percent certainty is possible. Ironically, an unreflective person is 100 percent certain of a lot more than a highly reflective one, because a highly reflective person eventually recognizes a number of "uncertainty principles," including these:

1. That the "laws of logic"—the software that thought runs on—must be accepted on faith, being unprovable (since you have to assume them in order to prove

them, which tends to not prove anything!): Thus all thought is ultimately based on a kind of faith!

2. That language has powerful effects on our experience of perceiving, thinking, and "knowing."

3. That the groups from which we derive our social identity (sociologists call them "plausibility structures") and our historical setting also have far-reaching effects on what we think we know.

4. That even our personality types — some of which seem by nature to be more questioning and others less so — affect how easily we are persuaded that we know the truth.

5. That at some point, practicality steps in: We are forced to answer a test question, or we have to decide whether to marry Lee or Terry, or we have to fund a project, or we have to get on with life — and doing so requires us to make some assumptions ... to decide that in spite of our lack of absolute certainty, we have to turn some things into "knowledge," which we call assumptions.

6. That sometimes even those assumptions have to be questioned.

Two Disclaimers

Let me interject with two disclaimers. First, I am not suggesting our elementary schools accept a divergence of opinion on multiplication tables, since some children who multiply thirteen by four and get fifty-seven may simply be working with different logic software! Rather, I am suggesting that we reflect more on how small (nonexistent?) is the sphere within which we actually "know" with complete, unassailable certainty. Second, I am not recommending the absurdities of "absolute relativism" or radical postmodernism—where we say that everything is relative and nobody can know anything with certainty, conveniently ignoring the fact that we seem to believe we know with complete certainty that everything is relative! To argue such a point is itself illogical: Why try to persuade you that my assertion is true if the point of the assertion is that there is no knowable truth? (We will return to this issue in chapter 8.)

No, rather than promoting relativism or a postmodern despair about being able to know or communicate truth, I am trying to push our thinking about our thinking beyond its normal limits because I believe that doing so can lead us to important insights about faith.

Revelation—a Solution?

Some of my believing friends feel they have solved the problem. The Bible (or the Gita or the Koran, or whatever), they say, provides direct revelation from God. Therefore, it is absolutely true and trustworthy, providing a sure foundation upon which all knowledge can be built. The Bible thus yields more than faith: It yields certainty, knowledge. Now you should know that I have great faith in the Bible, and have found it to have an importance and value for me above all other books, and I in fact used to be among those who thought the Bible solved the whole epistemological problem simply and cleanly, as many of my friends still think. But I can't follow that logic anymore. My own spiritual journey has presented me with questions that have reshaped (and continue to reshape) how I think about the Bible.

1. How do I know with absolute certainty that the Bible is the direct revelation of God? (And again, if I answer that, how do I know my ability to know is absolute and unflawed?) If I accept the authority of the Bible on any degree of faith, then the point has been made: we all live by faith, not certainty.

2. Even if I had complete certainty that the Bible was originally the direct revelation of God, how do I know with complete certainty that in all its copying, translations, and so forth, it has not been corrupted in some small ways? Even if the scope of the corruptions or uncertainties of translation is small, haven't I still lost absolute certainty?

3. Even if I had complete certainty that my translated copy of the fully inspired Bible were completely uncorrupted, or that the few corruptions were minor and insignificant, how do I know with complete certainty that my understanding of the document is absolutely complete and accurate? As soon as I acknowledge the potential for imperfections or misconceptions in my reading and interpretation (not to mention imperfections in its exposition and application by preachers), haven't I again lost absolute certainty?

4. Even if I were to concede all the previous questions (which, of course, I cannot), I am left with another even deeper question. Even if God—who as creator would probably know everything about everything—gave me a statement as simple as this: "I exist and I love you," could I fully grasp what the statement

means, with unassailable certainty that my understanding is accurate? Do I fully comprehend what God means when using the word "I"? Do I know what God would mean by the word "exist"—surely implying levels of existence far beyond what most of us have ever tried to imagine? What about the word "love"? Can I safely assume that a loving God will meet all my expectations, fulfill all my wishes, since I am loved? If not, what can I safely assume, and why?

Now again, I believe that the Bible has unique and immense value in our search for good faith and our search for God, and I don't want to be seen as someone who tries to discredit the Bible in any way. Rather, as someone who deeply respects the Bible, I think we do it a disservice by implying that it can do something that no book can. In spiritual matters as in used car sales, exaggerated claims may make a fast sale, but customers are soon dissatisfied, and eventually buyer's remorse sets in, along with a lasting distrust of the salesperson who overpromised and underdelivered. Promising absolute, unassailable certainty, even with the benefit of the Bible or any holy book, seems to be an exaggerated claim.

Do you begin to feel the magnitude of our question, "What is the relationship between faith and knowledge?"

A Level Playing Field

So where are we? As I have said before, we are left, the more reflective we become, with this realization: We are on a level playing field; none of us lives with absolute, unassailable certainty about anything; we all live by faith. What we might call practical certainty — the kind of certainty that allows us to ignore many of these rather abstract and far-fetched questions so we can get on with our lives — is really relative certainty, shot through with faith on many levels. Even the skeptic can only doubt one set of propositions because he believes another. Without some structure of faith, some plausibility structure, we can't get anywhere. We are like weightless, tractionless runners or boxers. We have no leverage. So, some degree of faith is downright inescapable, and faith runs through all we claim to know. (I realize that for some of us, this is such an immense realization that it seems trivial to say it so glibly. It might be best for some readers to put this book aside for a few days to let the dust settle, and see if you can really live with this conclusion.)

Faith and Knowledge

If it's any comfort, Albert Einstein reached a similar conclusion: In the words of Lesslie Newbigin (*The Gospel in a Pluralist Society*, Grand Rapids: Eerdmans, 1989, p. 33), "There is no knowing without believing, and believing is the way to knowing." Consider these quotes from Einstein:

> As far as the propositions of mathematics refer to reality, they are not certain; and as far as they are certain, they do not refer to reality.

> The supreme task of the physicist is the search for those highly universal laws from which a picture of the world can be obtained by pure deduction. There is no logical path leading to these laws. They are only to be reached by intuition, based upon something like an intellectual love.

The mechanics of discovery are neither logical nor intellectual. It's a sudden illumination, almost a rapture. Later, to be sure, intelligence and analysis and experiment confirm (or invalidate) the intuition. But initially there is a great leap of the imagination.

"A sudden illumination, rapture, intuition, intellectual love, a great leap of the imagination" ... they sound like the words of a poet or prophet, not a scientist. But those readers who are involved in science will likely agree: Science is a creative process involving many faculties in addition to cold, hard reason. (See chapter 5 for more on the super-rational dimensions to science.) The popular myths of objectivity and certainty notwithstanding, knowledge and belief need not be enemies, but can rather be partners in the search for truth.

What then is the relationship between faith and knowledge? What if faith, instead of being a step back from the limits of our ability to know and understand, could actually be a flight beyond the rim? What if the word "knowledge," used to denote certainty gained by rationalistic and empirical means, is actually only appropriate for mundane facts, pedestrian inquiries, common commodities? What if there is another category of reality in the universe, no less real just because it doesn't shrink itself to our instruments and portals of "knowledge"? What if that category of reality—let's call it mystery or spirituality—dwarfs all of our knowledge, as space dwarfs our little earth? Are we humble enough to look up from the little things we are so proud of comprehending and controlling, to face massive realities—humbling mysteries—greater than ourselves, and therefore greater than our ability to squeeze into our little boxes of "certainty" or "knowledge"? Are we willing to step off the narrow ledge of knowledge to soar into broad spaces of faith?

After all, as novelist Flannery O'Connor said, "Whatever you do anyway, remember that these things are mysteries and that if they were such that we could understand them, they wouldn't be worth understanding. A God you understood would be less than yourself."

Faith beyond Knowledge

I said earlier that in our postmodern times, we are increasingly aware of the limitations of human knowledge. We are aware perhaps as never before of the gap between what we subjectively "know" and what is objectively true. For people like us, boxed in little bodies with narrow portals of physical senses that are interpreted by fallible, limited (yet amazing!) little brains, absolute certainty is a gift we have not been given. We can only aspire to relative certainty, which involves relative uncertainty ... which leaves room for—no, more, which actually requires—faith.

We could content ourselves with petty pursuits and leave off any search for truth. But to do so feels cheap, for moral reasons if not for intellectual ones. So, into this profound human dilemma we go, needing to let go of certainty in order to reach for truth. We venture into this very real gap between our understanding "in here" and reality as it is "out there." We move into this territory where the limitations of knowledge are admitted and the value of seeking truth is also held high. Here, without faith we cannot go. It is the only vehicle we have.

We are faced again with the predicament we spoke of in the introduction, the predicament of being not just abstract note-takers gaining "knowledge" or information, but of people in a smoky building needing news of escape routes. We are faced again with the predicament we spoke of in chapter 1, of people needing to know if there is someone out there in the dark, beyond our ability to see. To call out, "Hello! Is anybody out there?" we have to act as if someone is there, even though we aren't sure. That is our human predicament, and that is the domain of faith.

I'm Sorry

I'm sorry. Beyond these musings, I can't map out for you a precise relationship between faith and knowledge. But I can tell you that I have looked at the question from many angles, and after all my considerations, I am more convinced than ever that faith is necessary, faith is inescapable, and good faith is a thing of great value — to find, to hold, to treasure, and to grow — if we aspire to seek the truth. The topic of the next chapter is how faith grows.

Your Response

Which statement best describes you?

I accept that everyone lives by faith to one degree or another.
I cannot yet accept this idea.
I am able to see faith as a step up from where I am now.
I am not yet able to see faith as a step up from where I am now.

Resources

Books that explore this topic from a vantage point of faith are, to date, rare. I expect this to change. By far the best religious thinker I have found in this regard to date is Lesslie Newbigin. See his *The Gospel in a Pluralist Society* or *The Open Secret*. Walker Percy's essay "The Message in the Bottle" is worth reading too (in his book *The Message in the Bottle*).

Fiction can perhaps explore this issue better than nonfiction. I recommend Orson Scott Card's Alvin Maker series, beginning with *Seventh Son*, and his Homecoming series beginning with *The Memory of Earth*. Card has the ability to show you the same reality from several vantage points, in a way that leads you to question the sole authority of your own vantage point in the real world.

Prayer

It is very humbling to face the limitations of my own certainty, my own knowledge. I do not want to rest on my own solitary powers of perception and reasoning, but neither do I want to discard them. Rather, I present all of my faculties of thinking and knowing, and hope to be guided through them ... and beyond them. My faith seeks understanding, and my understanding seeks faith. I see that humility is essential to pursuing faith, and that arrogance will sabotage my spiritual search. I aspire to have a truly intelligent faith, that is reason-plus, not reason-minus.

Chapter 3 Preview

How Does Faith Grow?

This chapter explores a four-stage model for the growth of faith. It suggests that as faith grows, one outgrows one stage and embraces a new stage, perhaps like growing out of and into new sizes of clothes or shoes. It suggests that this process is often painful, and summarizes my experience of progressing through the stages.

Who Should Read This Chapter?

This chapter is relevant to both the spiritual seeker who is still unsure of faith and the already-convinced person who has believed for many years.

What Questions Does It Address?

Why is the spiritual journey so often difficult? What are the characteristics of each of the four stages of faith development? How does doubt fit into the development of faith?

How Does Faith Grow?

I don't want to give you the impression that I live in this constant bliss of relative certainty about these matters of ultimate concern. Much of my spiritual life has been tortured by doubt. For example, when I see religious people act small, hypocritical, judgmental, violent, or even just plain nasty, the abandonment of faith becomes appealing. When I see suffering, poverty, and injustice, I sometimes find it easier to think that God does not exist than to think God can somehow let this go on for one more minute, even if God plans to rebalance the equation later. And in the middle of a bout of nausea or stomach cramps, frankly, I am not very sure of anything except that I wish I felt better.

Not everyone seems to experience the curse of doubt to the same degree, but those of us who are by nature reflective and who find doubt inescapable gradually must learn to see the curse as a mixed blessing. If I am able to help some readers work through their doubts and not be overcome by them, it is only because I have been there myself.

But even if there were no such consolations, there isn't any alternative to learning to deal with doubt. It is not as though I could simply give up my current faith and revert to another viewpoint that would never itself become doubtworthy! Even the convinced atheist, if he is the slightest bit reflective, has his doubts about atheism—whether they occur in a foxhole, hospice

of college life—where, for example, a human being is variously defined as a bag of evolving chemicals in biology class, a combination of integrated systems in anatomy class, a participant in class struggle or commodity consumption in economics class, an inhabitant of fictional realities in literature class, a seeker of pleasure or power in psychology class, a seeker of knowledge in philosophy class, and a seeker of God in her Sunday school class. She feels she must decide whether the biological view is correct, or the religious view is correct. In the process, she and her friends have many late-night philosophical debates. By her junior year, she may have become a fundamentalist, more sure of her religious beliefs than ever, or she may have "lost her faith" altogether. But even if she loses faith in religion, her newfound faith in science may be just as much a Stage One phenomenon.

Eventually, wearied by constant argument and either/or choices between worldviews, she soon "graduates" (or flunks out) of Simplicity and enters Stage Two: Complexity.

Now her aims are slightly more modest. She doesn't aspire to have all the easy answers: she rather hopes to get A's by figuring out how to play the various complex games—the biology game, the anatomy game, the economics game, and the psychology or philosophy or religion games, and so on. Now she seeks techniques by which to play the various complex games of adult life. She has given up on finding easy answers. What she hopes for now is methods, steps, instructions, and strategies for success. If Stage One was a game, it was the Right versus Wrong game, or the Us versus Them game; now in Stage Two, it's the Winners versus Losers game, the Success or Failure game. If in Stage One she wanted the right and good authority figures so that she could have as much absolute certainty about being absolutely right as possible, in Stage Two she wants coaches who will help her prevail over problems to be happy and successful as much of the time as possible.

Eventually, though, she may graduate from Stage Two, although graduation sometimes might feel like flunking out. Perhaps her techniques will fail her just as her easy answers did in Stage One, or perhaps she will feel a certain Stage-Two emptiness: that life has become "just a game" because that's the way she is playing it. Perhaps enough Stage One people will keep nagging her as an expression of their absolutism (the idea that their authority structure or belief system alone has the Right Answers that explain everything) that she becomes less comfortable in her pragmatism (the idea that "what works" is what matters). One way or another, Complexity gives way to Perplexity, maybe by her second year in graduate school. Now she may feel doubly disillusioned—first, disappointed in her search for Stage One easy answers, and now disappointed in her search for foolproof techniques. She may also feel bitter—angry at those authority figures who promised her easy answers and coached her in easy techniques, angry at the institutions of her childhood that made things seem so simple and easy. They all seem inauthentic and dishonest to her now, because she is beginning to see how little she or anyone really knows, how biased and self-serving everyone is, and how hard it can be to experience either honest knowing (Stage One's claim) or meaningful success (Stage Two's promise). Tempted as never before by cynicism and skepticism, she feels increasingly paralyzed and discouraged. Yet life makes demands of her, and the real world intrudes upon the ivory tower. She can't stay in graduate school forever!

She gradually realizes that she has developed some virtues and skills in the first three stages, and she draws on them to pick up the pieces and rebuild a coherent life. She lacks the naive arrogance and overconfidence that characterized her in Stage One and Stage Two, but now, chastened by Stage Three, she seeks to move ahead with a proper confidence into Stage Four: Humility.

These stages could be expanded as seen starting on page 77.

Moving through Stages

Clearly, people don't generally move out of or into a stage in one giant step. There are many hesitant explorations, retreats, renewed explorations. The transitions from infancy to childhood, childhood through puberty, adolescence through adulthood, and young adulthood to middle age certainly don't happen suddenly; a twelve-year-old is a child one minute, a young adult the next, it seems, then a child again, and so on. The same is true of these stages.

There is so much more we could say about these stages. For example, we could describe a Stage 0, where a person simply believes what he or she has been told and taught, without questioning, without even recognizing the possibility of questioning, without realizing there are any alternative beliefs or differing groups out there. We might add a Stage 5, where Stage 4 people specialize in helping people progress at their own pace through earlier stages. Or we could explore cultic behavior as a regressive step in this process, where, say, a young adult becomes intimidated by the complexities or perplexities of growing up in Stage 2 and throws himself into a Stage 1 group, against his better judgment, as a "bad faith" act of emotional desperation.

	Stage 1 Simplicity	Stage 2 Complexity	Stage 3 Perplexity	Stage 4 Humility
Focus	Right or wrong? Being right, belonging to the right group.	Effective or ineffective? Accomplishing, learning technique, winning.	Honest or dishonest? Authentic or inauthentic? Understanding, seeing through appearances and illusions to reality.	Wise or unwise? Fulfilling potential. Making the most of life.
Motive	Please authority figures; be an "insider."	Reach goals; be effective.	Be honest, authentic.	Make the best of opportunities. Serve, contribute, make a difference.
Beliefs	All truth is known or knowable. There are easy answers to every question. The right authority	Almost anything is doable. Different people have different methods, beliefs, approaches—the key is	All is questionable. Nothing is really certain, except uncertainty. Everything is relative.	There are a few basic absolute or universal truths, many relative matters, and much mystery.

	Stage 1 Simplicity	Stage 2 Complexity	Stage 3 Perplexity	Stage 4 Humility
	figures know the right answers.	finding the best ones.		There are enough basics to live by.
Perception	Dualistic, in terms of right versus wrong, good versus bad.	Pragmatic—looking for the useful, practical.	Relativistic, skeptical.	Integrated, synthesizing the dualism, pragmatism, and relativism of earlier stages.
Mottos	You are either for us or against us; it's all or nothing.	There is more than one way to do things—find whatever works best for you.	Everyone's opinion is equally valid and equally questionable. Who knows who really is right?	I will focus on a few grand essentials. In essentials, unity; in nonessentials, diversity; in all things, charity.
Authorities	Godlike. God's representatives, with divine right.	Coaches. They help you grow.	Demonic. They are dishonest controllers, trying	People like you and me—imperfect, doing their

best, sometimes admirable and dependable, sometimes untrustworthy and despicable, sometimes sincerely misguided. We like people who combine thoughtfulness with accomplishment.	to impose easy answers on complex realities. We like other questioners, free spirits, and nonconformists. We dislike people in Stages 1 and 2.	We like people who give clear instructions and let us know what they expect of us. We like people who motivate us and make us feel like doing things. We dislike people	They help you know. **Like/Dislike** We like bold, clear, assertive, confident people who know the answers. We dislike tentative, qualifying, timid, or unsure people who say, "I don't know."

	Stage 1 Simplicity	Stage 2 Complexity	Stage 3 Perplexity	Stage 4 Humility
		who are too dogmatic (Stage 1) or mystical (Stage 3).		
Life Is	A war.	A complex game. You have to learn the rules.	A joke or a mystery or a search.	A mixture: what you make it; what it is.
Strategy	Learn the answers. Learn what to think. Learn to identify and avoid "the enemy."	Learn the technique. Play the game. Find what people want and give it to them.	Ask hard questions. Be ruthlessly honest.	Learn all the answers and techniques you can (Stages 1 and 2), ask all the questions you can (Stage 3), and try to fulfill your potential, admitting how little you really know.

Strengths	High commitment, a willingness to sacrifice and suffer for the cause.	Enthusiasm, idealism, action.	Depth, honesty, often humor or artistic sensitivity.	Many strengths of earlier stages, plus stability, endurance, wisdom, and humility.
Weaknesses	Willing to kill or inflict suffering for the cause. Arrogant, simplistic, combative, judgmental, intolerant. Incapable of distinguishing major from minor issues, since every issue is part of a rigid system that has embraced all (as universal, absolute, and iner-	Superficial, naive. Critical of those who aren't successful. Insecure about one's own success—prone to brag or name-drop. May imitate successful others and seem inauthentic—playing a role or game. May try or push too hard or be too competitive.	Cynical, uncommitted, withdrawn, depressed, or elitist.	May display weaknesses of earlier stages.

	Stage 1 Simplicity	Stage 2 Complexity	Stage 3 Perplexity	Stage 4 Humility
	rant) or nothing (as false, wrong, discredited).			
Identity	Found in my leader or group.	Found in a cause or achievement.	Found in solitude or a small circle of similarly alienated friends.	Found in my relationship to the whole, or to God.
Relationships	Dependent or codependent, willing to take orders from respected authority.	Increasingly independent, eager to play special role on team.	Counter-dependent, critical.	Interdependent, collaborative, empathetic.
God Is	The Ultimate Authority Figure and/or Ultimate Friend.	The Ultimate Guide or Coach.	Either a mythic authority figure I have outgrown, an opiate of the	Knowable in part, yet mysterious; present, yet transcendent; just, yet

merciful. (Being able to hold dynamic tensions about God.)

That this is the last stage in our schema doesn't suggest that one lives happily ever after! At this stage of integration, one now faces all the weaknesses of the previous stages. Whenever one enters a new context (a new career, a new religion, a new social

masses, or a mystery I am seeking.

Stage 3 is a struggle between arrogance ("Those simpletons in Stages 1 and 2 don't see how shallow and primitive they are! Ha! They've never even asked the questions we ask, much less found answers for them! Ha!") and humility. And there is

Three problems push people out of Stage 2 (usually against their will). First, the prevalence of Stage 1 people always claiming to have all the answers prohibits Stage 2 people from escaping questions about truth. Second, the failure of "foolproof" tech-

As Stage 1 people encounter diversity in their ranks, or are disillusioned because of fallen leaders or internal squabbles in the group from which they derive their identity, or are unsettled by the multiplicity of viewpoints, they tend to swing from a desire for

Transition

Stage 1 Simplicity	Stage 2 Complexity	Stage 3 Perplexity	Stage 4 Humility
internal knowledge and certainty to a desire for external accomplishment and success, thus moving on to Stage 2. The world isn't simple anymore, so the task changes—to make life work in this complex environment.	niques and projects leaves them disillusioned and perplexed—prime characteristics of Stage 3. Third, Stage 2 people survive by fragmenting complex and apparently contradictory truth into categories (scientific truth, religious truth, social or relational truth, political truth).	much in this stage to humble a person. Notably, one has to get on with life, and life requires one to make commitments, and commitments grow out of values and beliefs, so one is not left with the option of staying in limbo. One has to make choices. One can't blindly accept a group's or	network), he or she may well recapitulate the stages repeatedly. After all, humility, like maturity, is obviously not a destination, but rather a journey in itself.

Eventually, a desire for unity and integration causes them to be dissatisfied with their fragmented approach.	authority figure's agenda anymore, but one has to take responsibility for living life — chastened and more realistic, often disillusioned and less idealistic — in short, humble.	

Or we could consider how different religions, churches, denominations, or religious organizations (or even nations and civilizations) have a corporate identity in one stage or another. We could look at the belief systems, practices, or structures that encourage or impede development, and identify the reasons groups often enfranchise and serve people at one stage, but may harm or reject people at others. That could open up some fascinating considerations of how organizations can better serve people through the whole process, and how organizations can themselves go through the stages with self-awareness. Or we could consider the different ways that people at various stages approach the Bible or other sacred writings, as the Book of Easy Answers and Absolutes for Stage 1, as the Spiritual How-To Manual for Stage 2, either as an outmoded tool of oppression by Stage 1 authority figures or as a refreshingly diverse and honest artifact for Stage 3 folk, or as a library for lifelong learning for those in Stage 4.

But our focus here is on the finding of faith and the growing of faith — which ironically can feel like losing faith.

Here is how growing in faith can feel like losing faith entirely: When a person begins to outgrow Stage 1 faith, it feels like doubt. Then, appropriating a Stage 2 faith feels like finding faith again — and that feeling of satisfaction and renewal lasts until Stage 3 is knocking at the door. Most people don't know there is a more advanced stage waiting outside the door, so to them, this knocking feels dreadful, disloyal, dangerous. Most of us fight it and try to avoid answering the door as long as possible. If we welcome the intruder of doubt or dissatisfaction or new questions in, it feels like the end of faith for us, not the beginning of a new stage. Even when Stage 4 knocks, Stage 3 usually only lets go after a fight.

My Background

I have seen this pattern play out in my own life. I was brought up in a very conservative Christian group. For most people in this group, the world was created in six twenty-four-hour periods, less than ten thousand years ago. Species did not evolve, but were formed from clay by the literal hands of God. Adam and Eve literally ate a literal forbidden fruit, and that one act explains literally everything that is wrong with the world today. Noah's flood covered every square inch of planet earth. All other religions — including most "Christian" denominations — were simply wrong, from the devil, many hell-bound. Women must never speak in church (although they may sing and teach children) and should let their husbands rule the home. Philosophy and science were evil; studying them was a waste of time (or worse) compared to studying the Bible. For that reason, higher education was often suspect. Why get all that godless learning when the world is going to end any day anyway?

Now before you react too strongly, let me say that there were many wonderful people (my parents among them) in the church of my childhood — exactly the kind of people you would want for your boss, employee, neighbor, fishing buddy, or golf partner. The sincerity of devotion and genuine neighborliness of many of the "saints" there was among the most beautiful and poignant I have ever seen. Let me also say that the dogmatism of many "secular" families, in opposite ways, of course, can be just as "fundamentalist" as the devotion of religious families. But let me also say that this kind of environment was impossible for a boy of my reflective temperament — there wasn't room there for a person like me.

Stage 1 Doubt

I am by nature a questioner. I can't help it. I have a built-in urge to ask questions, and to me, experts earn their credibility by their willingness to be tested or doubted. In addition, from before first grade, when my dad would sit next to me on the sofa reading books about nature, I have been an incurable book-lover. By the time I was in seventh grade, I had memorized the Latin genus and species name of nearly every North American reptile, not because I was trying to, but simply because I was by that time reading college-level textbooks on herpetology ... my great boyhood passion (until I discovered girls and the fact that girls were not interested in that sort of thing generally).

In all of that reading, it was inevitable that I would start questioning the dogma of my church. At first, this questioning had to do with the specifics of my denomination: "Why do we think we are so right and all other Christians are so wrong?" But by the time I was fourteen or so, I was wondering if the whole God-thing was a hoax. Perhaps my secular scientific education had it right after all.

This is a classic Stage 1 dichotomy: There are good guys and bad guys, and maybe the guys I thought were good (church people) were really the bad guys, and the bad guys (scientists, intellectuals) were really the good guys. I was questioning who really wore the white hats, but I wasn't questioning my view of the world in which everyone fit into one of two categories.

Enter Stages 2 and 3

I had some very powerful spiritual experiences and influences in my teenage years that convinced me that I couldn't simply reject God. I was on a few occasions brought to tears of joy and gratitude when I felt—you might say intuitively, or perhaps mystically—the magnitude of God's love and utter beauty. Sometimes this occurred in response to the natural world, to watching the stars or considering the order, harmony, diversity, and vigor of an ecosystem. Sometimes I felt that I was encountering God in other people—people who seemed to arrive in my life just at the right time, as if sent by God.

I also came across some intelligent Christian writers and thinkers by my senior year of high school (C. S. Lewis, Francis Schaeffer, and others) who gave me some hope that a person didn't have to check his or her brains at the door when entering church. So, having been confirmed in my Christian commitment, I turned my focus from which tribe I was going to join and which authorities I was going to follow to how to make this thing called the Christian life work. This was my entry into Stage 2 faith—preoccupied with how-to's, techniques, practicalities: How do I learn more of the Bible? How do I pray more? How do I get along with my parents better? How do I relate to people better? How do I find God's will for my life—in my career choice and college choice and dating choices? How do I deal with my sexuality? How do I find more happiness? How do I find more success?

That preoccupation lasted into my college years. But during college, Stage 2 faith began to falter. Stage 3 was knocking at the door, and it was knocking hard. I was an English major, and deconstruction, postmodernism, relativism, pluralism, and all their cousins made my Stage 2 version of Christianity seem more and more like a tacky infomercial on late-night cable TV. Sure, some people have bought it, and it works for some people, but is it really true and right for everybody? Aren't the claims hyped up, exaggerated, falsified by group dynamics? Isn't my "brand" of faith just one of many on the market, in no way superior to anyone else's? Granted, those making the assault on my faith (professors, fellow students, writers) didn't have it together themselves. It wasn't that they had a better lifestyle or better answers, but their cynicism and skeptical tone were enough to make me lose Stage 2 faith by my senior year.

Stage 3 Struggles

I was fortunate at this time to have good friends who weren't put off by my spiritual malaise, people who gave me room to question and doubt. I remember unloading with one of them, Tom Willett, about the erosion of my faith and my mountain of questions, and then Tom saying something like this: "Brian, I can tell your faith is shaky right now, but my faith is strong, and I just want you to know that reality doesn't look so gloomy for me. God doesn't seem very real to you, but God is very real to this person you know and trust sitting across the room from you." For him to keep faith in God and our friendship meant a lot to me. I also remember him offering me some hope: "As your worldview expands to grapple with all the things you're thinking about, you will have a perspective much broader than that of most people. You will be able to help a lot of other people in some pretty deep ways because of what you're going through now." That didn't solve the problem, but it gave me hope that a solution would be worthwhile, if it ever came.

Stage 3 was hard on me and lasted a long time. I wrote a song in those days that conveys Stage 3 pretty clearly. In the song, God is still present, but only as a glimmer on the periphery of sight, like Moses' burning bush, but barely visible. Paradoxically, there is a sense of drifting, disillusionment, and alienation, along with a sense of clarity, liberation from "false security," and revelation. Stage 3 doesn't look like faith from "the inner circle" of Stage 1 and 2 perspectives, but there can be real faith there nonetheless. Here is the song, called "Sunken Corner":

> It's a rainy night. The streets are shining like a carnival
> with colored lights:
> flashing red and blinking yellow, neon blue and mellow
> sodium white.
> I cannot see the lines they've painted. I'm trying to find
> the lane where I belong.
> So if you see me drifting, mister, it's just the weather. I
> ain't done nothing wrong.
> So meet me at the sunken corner. I know a diner there
> that's light and cool and clean.
> While we taste our toast and coffee, we can relate illu-
> sions that we've seen.
> I feel the blaze of revelation, I feel the stir of inspiration
> rumbling.
> It's a process of elimination, an interruption to our con-
> versation. It's coming. . . .
> I have some friends snug in the inner circle. You couldn't
> pay them to exchange their place with you or me.
> But at least we have this consolation: There's not much
> here in the way of false security.
> You find God in the strangest places, places you would
> never choose to be.
> I feel like Moses on the mountain: It's burning
> there—what can I do but see?
> What can I do but see?

Stage 3 was for me a time of simply trying to keep my eyes open — to see evidences for God and to see questions and issues my faith couldn't explain or handle (most significantly, the apparent pigheadedness and bad taste of so many Christians whose faith was supposed to make a positive difference in their lives, but too often didn't). I sometimes wondered if my faith would survive. But it did. Chastened, seasoned, pruned, tested, humbled. That is what Stage 4 faith is all about.

Stage 4 Frontiers

I remained more or less in Stage 3 through graduate school. If there was one catalyst that helped me get beyond Stage 3, it was my graduate work on novelist Walker Percy. Percy was an adult convert to Roman Catholicism. He had his dark side, his doubts and depressions, but he exemplified in his novels and essays an approach to Christianity that was more stable, more humble, more honest, more thoughtful, full of more intellectual integrity, than anything I had seen in my Protestant evangelical circles. It was a Christianity unlike the fundamentalism of my childhood (too often defined, I felt, largely by its reaction against and retreat from modernity) and unlike the liberal Christianity of the mainline churches (too often defined, I felt, largely by its capitulation to and endorsement of modernity). Instead, it was a Christianity engaged with modernity (and postmodernity) — grappling with its issues, sensitive to its questions and concerns, aware of its spiritual vacuum, in vital dialogue with its artistic and intellectual leaders. It was a "third-way" faith seeking to steer a course that would avoid defensive retreat and isolation on the one hand and capitulation and sell-out on the other.

The faith that I have been learning and growing and seeking to live out during the twenty years since then has been of this Stage 4 type. I never would have gotten there without the first three stages, but the first three stages alone never would have brought me to where I am today.

Rough Riding

But again, I don't want to give you the impression that Stage 4 has been a gentle ride, free of hairpin curves, potholes, and roadside breakdowns. Far from it. In fact, I have seen myself repeat the cycle, repeatedly going through all four stages in more or less dramatic ways, recapitulating the journey in a kind of widening spiral again and again, through simplicity, complexity, and perplexity to new levels of humility. That is what mature faith requires—not pride over how much one sees and understands, but humility, the feeling that one is still a child, certain of so little, still so dependent on God and others, with so much still to learn—including so much more to learn about humility. Philosophers sometimes talk about two simplicities, a bold, naive one on this side of complexity and a humbled, seasoned one on the other side. That describes the process pretty well, I think.

Even in Stage 4 faith, there are occasional mornings I wake up and look in the mirror and think, "Have I been a fool to live for things I can't see, instead of going after money and comfort and pleasure like many other people?" Once, when I was the speaker for a large youth retreat, I spent all the time between my messages wondering, "Do I myself really believe in God anymore?"

At those times, my faith seeks deeper understanding. My faith looks for evidence, for good reasons to keep on believing. I know that logic and reason won't force me to believe, but I also have learned that clear thinking can often help me to believe. So, to questions of God's existence and character we will turn in the next several chapters, looking for good reasons to believe.

For those of you at a transition between stages, these chapters might help your faith stretch to the next level. For those of you approaching faith for the first time, this logical approach may remove obstacles, shorten the distance between where you are and where you want to be, and thus make the first step into faith more manageable.

Your Response

1. In which of the four stages do you see yourself now?
2. What transitions/challenges should you expect ahead in the road?

Prayer

I may not be sure if anyone is there to listen to what I am saying. I may even feel a bit silly saying these words. But if there is a good, kind, compassionate God able to hear me, I have to believe that these words will be interpreted as a sincere attempt at prayer and as an expression of whatever small amount of faith I have. I hope that if I am being heard, I will be helped and guided and that the thinking stimulated by this book will be of value to me.

Part 2

Thinking about God

Can I **Believe in Atheism**?

This chapter addresses the question, "Is there a God?" and considers the first possible answer: no, the answer of atheism. It suggests that many atheists have good reasons for their belief and explores those reasons. It also suggests a number of reasons for moving beyond atheism to consider the other possible answers. It argues that atheism is a belief just as theism is.

Who Should Read This Chapter?

If you are a committed atheist, this chapter will probably not convince you to become a believer in God overnight. It will, I hope, nudge you to reopen the question of God's existence and continue your search. If you are not a committed atheist, but have frequent or occasional doubts about the existence of God, this chapter will help you understand what is at stake in foreclosing on the possibility of God's existence.

What Questions Does It Address?

Why do some people choose atheism? Why is atheism a matter of faith just as much as theism? Why should people move beyond atheism?

Shake off all the fears of servile prejudices, under which weak minds are servilely crouched. Fix reason firmly in her seat, and call on her tribunal for every fact, every opinion. Question with boldness even the existence of a God; because, if there be one, he must more approve of the homage of reason than that of blindfolded fear.

Thomas Jefferson

4

Can I **Believe in Atheism?**

Our quest for faith now brings us to this blunt, stark question: Is there a God? Why waste our time searching for something/someone that does not really exist? Let's abandon from the start the quest for a faith that is comforting but delusional. I agree with C. S. Lewis: "Comfort is one thing you cannot get by looking for it. If you look for truth, you may find comfort in the end: If you look for comfort you will not get either comfort or truth—only soft soap and wishful thinking to begin with and, in the end, despair."

So, is there a God? Three answers present themselves when we raise this question: No, I don't know, and yes. We will consider the first answer in this chapter.

The "no" answer is the atheist position. Now it must be granted that this answer is a position of faith, because no one can prove conclusively that God doesn't exist. Consider this diagram:

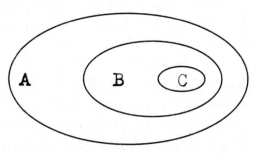

99

Let figure A represent all truth everywhere. (Obviously, these figures aren't drawn to any scale!) Let figure B represent the sum of all truth known by all human beings. And let figure C represent the knowledge of the person answering no to our question.

Granted, this person can honestly say, "No, in my experience, I recognize the existence of no God." But for this person to deny the huge quantity of experience of the vast majority of other humans through all of history—nearly all of whom say they have experienced God in some way—and to extend his certainty even beyond the realm of all human experience to figure A, saying that no God exists anywhere out there, even beyond human experience ... I think you will agree that this is a statement beyond knowledge, beyond certainty, beyond science, and beyond logic. It is a statement of faith.

That doesn't mean the atheist is wrong. It does mean, again, that the playing field is level. The atheist does not have the high ground of logic, reason, science, knowledge, and certainty, as some people seem to feel, leaving the unenlightened masses to muddle along in faith. No, as we have already seen, theists and atheists alike live by faith of one sort or another.

The fact is, there are strong reasons for making a faith commitment to the atheist position. If we could peel back the surface layers, beneath the "no" answer of many atheists we would find some strong reasons like these:

1. All or nearly all religious people I have met are kooks. I find them repulsive, ill-mannered, naive, or unintelligent. I don't want to be associated with them, and I can distance myself by self-identifying as an atheist.

2. I feel that religion is a primitive feature of immature civilization that must be outgrown. I wish to align myself with the progressive edge of human evolution—hence my atheism.

3. I have chosen a scientific worldview, which prohibits me from believing in anything that can't be verified by either my senses or a mathematical proof.

4. I have certain sexual, moral, or relational practices that would be inconsistent with any belief in God and its attendant morality. I prefer to avoid internal tension and qualms of conscience by excluding God rather than by reevaluating my behavior. I wouldn't want to be a hypocrite by professing a belief that is denied by my actions.

5. I am busy having fun, making money, meeting potential sexual partners, drinking or using drugs, or being otherwise amused, and I frankly don't have the time or energy to consider believing in God, so I reject the possibility as a convenience.

6. I have thoroughly examined the evidence, and I found it less than compelling, so I have made my choice on the "innocent until proven guilty" premise: Without compelling proof to the contrary, I will believe the universe exists innocent of any deity.

7. I used to be very religious, but I had such horrible experiences with belief that I rejected it as an act of self-preservation.

8. I believed in God, but experiences of suffering, injustice, and evil have prompted me to conclude that God must not exist.

9. I watched God evaporate or become obsolete. God was frequently called in to explain mysterious phenomena in life—disease, "acts of God" like floods, tornadoes, or earthquakes. But in each case, other explanations became known

(bacteria, genetics, El Niño, cold fronts, plate tectonics), and so the "God of the gaps" had no gaps left to fill.

At least some of these reasons, I am sure you will agree, seem valid. True, they may not be logically watertight, but they sound like the kinds of reasons people give to make other life decisions — like choosing or leaving a career, marrying or divorcing a spouse, and so forth. Many pastors have learned to make this request when people tell us they don't believe in God: "Tell me about the God you don't believe in." Usually, when people describe the God they have rejected, we can say, "I agree with you! I couldn't believe in that sort of God either." Then we try to help them see that there are ways to believe in God other than the way they have rejected.

Any of these reasons might do for you, however, if you want to choose, by faith, atheism as your life option. If you have already chosen it, of course, you have little reason to continue with this book. Otherwise, I hope you will consider the other two options (agnosticism and theism) before making a final decision.

Following are six good reasons — better reasons, I think — for bypassing the "no" answer.

1. If There Is No God, "The Big Questions" Remain Unanswered

Where does everything come from? Why does something exist rather than nothing? Why did the Big Bang bang when it did and how did it? Why did conscious, intelligent life develop? Does life have meaning? Does human history lead anywhere, or is it all in vain? Is death the end? Are good and evil, right and wrong ultimate realities, or mere social constructs, human opinions?

Now you might be saying in answer to these "big questions": "Who needs a reason or explanation? Evolution. Chance. Time. It all just happened. It's here. Who cares why or with what meaning?"

Part of me wants to point out that this kind of response can be as facile as the platitudes of many religious folk who answer every question with an unthinking, "The Lord works in mysterious ways" or "Just have faith" or some such statement. It can be a lazy excuse for not thinking; it can be a casual brushing off of a matter of ultimate concern.

Part of me wants to say that, but part of me wants to say nothing. After all, if you are completely content in an atheistic worldview, and the big questions don't seem important to you, or if they seem easily answerable with your current God-free data, then there's not much I can say. I might ask, "What circumstances would serve to make you open to other answers?" But I certainly can't push you in a direction you don't want to go. You are free to stop right here if you prefer, and I will be one of the first to stand to defend your right and freedom to do just that.

Possible Explorations

But if you are open to moving farther in this search, there are a number of directions we could explore to assure you that God is still a credible hypothesis when facing life's big questions. For example, many people find themselves reconsidering God's existence through the study of cosmology (the origin of everything). They ask: If the Second Law of Thermodynamics is true, if everything tends to run down, to cool, to decompose (i.e., to experience entropy), and if the universe has always existed, why wouldn't it have run down already, reaching a steady state of maximum entropy? Clearly, we find ourselves in the middle of a story with a real beginning. Recent discoveries in cosmic background radiation and star formation and decay confirm that conclusion, pointing to a genesis point for the universe some fifteen billion years ago. Again, people ask: Why did everything that is pop into existence? And even more: Why did it pop into existence so amazingly calibrated to make stars possible, and planets possible, and organic compounds possible, and life possible on at least one planet—an amazing series of feats that, the more we learn, become more and more astounding? The old ideas of a Prime Mover and Intelligent Designer begin to seem plausible again.

The classic "argument from design" is not only alive and well; more, some would say—it is making a strong comeback after being temporarily discredited by the now-discredited steady state and oscillating universe theories. "If the universe is like a clock, there must be someone like a clockmaker," the argument from design asserts, or "If the universe is like a symphony, there must be someone like a composer," or "If the universe is like a thought, there must be something like a mind."

Please don't misunderstand me: I have no desire to stir up old creation-evolution debates. I am all for letting those sleeping dogs rest in peace! True, many intelligent people have found the evolutionary model incapable of explaining the appearance of complex systems: the eye, reproductive organs, blood capabilities, brains, and other "black boxes," to use Michael Behe's term (*Darwin's Black Box: The Biochemical Challenge to Evolution*, New York: Free Press, 1996). These and other problems in traditional Darwinism (such as the reality of "punctuated equilibrium" reflected in the fossil record) have led some to propose an "anthropic principle"—that the universe somehow conspires to produce intelligent life, that life itself is a fundamental reality like matter and energy, that natural selection may indeed have an intelligent supernatural Selector working behind the scenes to help it along. Nancy Pearcy, a philosopher of science, puts it like this:

> Darwin's purpose was to show that the design in living things was only apparent and could be explained by something other than intelligent design. Darwin's argument sounded plausible, it was worth investigating, but it hasn't worked. There is an irreducible complexity in living things that is not explainable by any mechanistic view. ("I Believe," ed. Howard Means, *The Washingtonian*, December 1997, p. 101)

But I am still nervous about trumpeting unanswered questions about Big Bang cosmology and problems with Darwinism as evidence for the existence of God. I have seen people of faith make the same mistake too often: appealing to "the gaps" in scientific knowledge as evidence for God's existence, only to find those gaps erased or shrunk as scientific knowledge increases. The "God of the Gaps" project seems like a risky, already-been-tried endeavor to me. For example, Stephen Hawking's Wave Function theory already offers an alternative answer to the "who set off the Big Bang?" question, and some, at least, find the theory satisfying. Regarding Darwinism, I wouldn't be surprised if other "nonmiraculous" mechanisms are discovered that handle the current difficulties in biological evolution. Whether or not life evolves, science does, and its track record for finding natural causes or explanations for supposed supernatural events is impressive indeed.

That is why I am more interested in the evidence for God seen in what we know than I am in the supposed evidence to be found in what we don't know. To me, finding a "natural explanation" for something seems irrelevant to whether there is a God or not.

Two Evolutions

I know that many religious people have set up creation and evolution as enemies, basically forcing you to choose either their antievolutionary version of theism, or evolution-and-atheism as a package deal. I don't see it that way at all. As I explained in an earlier book (*The Church on the Other Side*, Grand Rapids: Zondervan, 1998), if by the term *evolution* we mean a purely natural, unplanned, undesigned, accidental, mindless mechanism that explains the development of everything (including life and consciousness) within an airtight system of physics and chemistry (without God or Spirit or transcendent meaning) by impersonal randomness plus time plus nothing—then of course, we are looking at an irreconcilable enemy to theism. In this view, evolution is an uncreated, self-existent, and universal principle or force that "selects" and "leads" toward complexity and even intelligence. It starts to look like a god itself, leaving the position filled and leaving any other aspiring deities standing in the unemployment line outside of reality.

But if by the term *evolution* we mean simply an observation of adaptive development from simple to complex, a pattern of change suggested by the data of the fossil record, an elegant process involving adaptation through inherent flexibility and survival of the fittest, then we have something potentially very different from an enemy to theism. We have one of the possible means by which God created. As such, the evolutionary process can be seen not as an enemy of theism, but rather as a creation of God, and a grand one at that. In this view, it would be a creation intended to produce other creations, a "natural" tool designed and used by a supernatural God, a creative process or tool (such as erosion or plate tectonics) for producing planet earth as we know it, another great reason to admire and even worship God rather than doubt or disbelieve.

There are others more qualified than I to guide you deeper into these subjects, but I simply mention them here to support my recommendation that you keep your mind open on the existence of God, rather than close it prematurely. For now, I hope you will agree that it's no sin to have an open mind to at least consider the big questions, and to keep open the option that God might be part of the answer.

2. If We Reject the Existence of God, We Are Left with a Crisis of Meaning

Perhaps you have heard of Jean-Paul Sartre and his fellow thinkers of the existentialist school in the early twentieth century. Although I don't share their choice of atheism, I applaud their honesty when dealing with the question of the existence of God. If he were alive, Sartre might say something like this: "The difference between us existentialists and other intellectuals is this: They all say that God doesn't exist and it doesn't matter, while we say that God doesn't exist and it makes all the difference."

Many of the existentialists explored, with courage and sensitivity, what it means to live in a godless world. Take Sartre's character Antoine Roquentin, for example, in *Nausea*. Roquentin sits on a park bench and sees a root descending from a chestnut tree behind the bench into the ground between his feet. But he thinks (I'm paraphrasing), "What is 'root' but a term I use to distinguish some stuff from other stuff? The word is merely a construct my mind artificially imposes on reality, not a real quality of existence itself." And as he lets the word "root" go, he sees the root-stuff blend in with the surrounding dirt-stuff. But it doesn't stop there. His experience expands into a kind of deconstructing vision where everything—the bench he sits on, the feet below him, the body to which they are attached, all trees, all people, everything—all are stripped of their categories and names and reduced to meaningless stuff. The experience overwhelms him with nausea.

The Will to Meaning

That is where the most sensitive and thoughtful among us find ourselves when we come to grips with what it means to live in a world without God. The universe is just stuff, expanding and contracting in space and time, going nowhere, meaning nothing, random noise echoing like gibberish, like nonsense words spoken by nobody to nobody with no intent. Maybe on a good day when the stock market is up and our teeth aren't aching, we can avoid such melancholy conclusions. But when war breaks out, or the lab tests come back positive, or the dreaded phone call comes, something in us—or at least, in most of us—cries out that life should have some purpose, meaning, direction, point. Victor Frankl said it like this: "The will to meaning is really a specific need not reducible to other needs, and is in greater or smaller degree present in all human beings" (*The Unheard Cry for Meaning*, New York: Washington Square Press, 1985, p. 33).

Take Franz Kafka's Gregor Samsa in *The Metamorphosis*. The poor chap, a traveling salesman, wakes up one morning to find himself transformed into a cockroach. The story is told with such droll matter-of-factness as to make one laugh. But like Roquentin, Samsa is facing the reality that if there is no God, then there is no transcendence above stuff, above insectness, above meaninglessness.

To move from fiction to autobiography, consider Leo Tolstoy's *A Confession*. The young Tolstoy began asking questions, as many young people do, about the meaning of his life:

> "Well," I said to myself, "I know everything that science so much wants me to know, but this path will not lead me to an answer to the question of the meaning of my life."... The answer given by this branch of knowledge to my question about the meaning of my life was only this:... You are a little lump of something randomly stuck together.... The lump decomposes. The decomposition of this lump is known as your life. The lump falls apart, and thus the decomposition ends, as do all your questions. Thus the clear side of knowledge replies, and if it strictly follows its own principles, there is no more to be said.... To say that [my life] is a particle of infinity not only fails to give it any meaning but destroys all possible meaning. (New York: Norton, 1983, pp. 41–42)

Perhaps you can live with that kind of answer. But don't let yourself off too easily. What happens if millions of people share this nihilism (the belief that everything is ultimately meaningless)? Consider: What if it is really true that we are just stuff, just lumps of protoplasm, products of blind, mechanical accidents with no design or destiny, pathetic organisms cursed with consciousness, with silly illusions of meaning and values and morality and beauty and art and all the rest, when really we are no different from insects, just blind urges destined to burn out, just fermenting lumps, just stuff swirling in stuff? What would the effects of that belief be, not only on you, but on the world, if millions of people actually believed it? That leads to our third reason for considering the nonatheistic options.

3. If People Don't Believe in God, the Historical Results Can Be Horrific

John Lennon encouraged us, in his classic song "Imagine," to envision a world where happy people live free of the tyranny of belief in God. He invited us to imagine "there's no heaven ... no hell below us, above us only sky," to picture "all the happy people living for today ... living life in peace," to envision a world with "nothing to kill or die for and no religion too." Such a world would "be as one," he promised.

The song is beautiful, and it is aptly titled, because you do have to imagine such a world: Reality (so far) offers no actual examples to examine. Quite the reverse. The bitter regimes of the twentieth-century's Hitlers, Stalins, Pol Pots, and their colleagues held as their core ideology overt or covert atheistic assumptions. Religion was the problem, they felt; eradicate it, and we can get on with helping the world "be as one." Imagine if they had succeeded! David Putnam's *The Killing Fields*, Steven Speilberg's *Schindler's List*, William Golding's *Lord of the Flies*, or Quentin Tarrantino's *Pulp Fiction* offer imaginative looks at human culture uncoupled from substantial faith, views more in line with reality than John Lennon's hauntingly beautiful song.

Please don't misunderstand me. I am not naive about the terrible atrocities and follies committed by the religious, as a number of my other books make clear. (For example, see *A Generous Orthodoxy* [Zondervan, 2004], especially chapter 18.) In fact, I agree with Lennon that we would be better off without some kinds of religion and some concepts of heaven. I am suggesting that when a society doesn't have a good and healthy faith, it experiences a meaning and values vacuum, and that vacuum will generally be filled by something undesirable—most often, I think, the dual pursuit of pleasure and power. When a society (atheistic or religious) sees pleasure or power as its ultimate end, things seem pretty consistently to go south for it, and its people can't seem to sustain the long-term will to be good, at least, not in sufficient numbers to keep themselves from slipping into nightmarish moral and social decay.

Again, please don't misunderstand me: I am not saying you should choose your belief based on its outcome. I am not recommending that you say, "Theism must be true because the practical effects of atheism are so unsavory." That is a logical leap I wouldn't encourage anyone to take. Rather, in light of the practical personal and social implications of atheism—the real ones, not the ones you have to imagine—it is wise not to close the door too fast on theism. Although something is not necessarily true because it "works" or false because it doesn't "work," if something doesn't work, if it consistently produces disastrous personal and social consequences, its impracticality may signal a philosophical "design failure" of some sort. That is why, as much as I love the aspiration of John Lennon's great song, in the end I still think the atheistic utopia he describes will always be ... imaginary.

4. If There Is No God, the Problems of Evil and Suffering Are in No Way Solved

True, if you do believe in God, you are left with "the problem of evil": How can an all-good, all-powerful God allow evil and suffering to exist in a universe he/she creates and controls? In the face of this profound question, some feel they can "solve the problem" by removing God. Such desperation is understandable when victims of rape, torture, oppression, natural catastrophe, random accident, or devastating disease raise their fists to heaven crying, "Why? Why?" One can't help but sympathize with the grief and rage that lead to this rejection of God.

But what is one left with, having removed the God-factor from the equation? Now, the suffering is no less tragic. And worse, there is now no hope of the suffering being rendered meaningful or transcendent, redemptive or redeemable, since no interventions in this life or reparations in an afterlife are possible. True, there is no God to blame, but is that so great a consolation? Neither is there a God to reach out to for strength and comfort and a higher perspective. There is no God to make meaning of the madness; there is only madness. Not a good trade, in my opinion.

I don't say this glibly. As a pastor, I am often the person people come to see when tragedy strikes. I hear their stories, feel their rage, empathize with their doubts. And I have been there too. It is common and natural to want to blame God in suffering, at the very least to echo Jesus' own words, "My God, my God, why have you forsaken me?" But removing God via atheism solves little and costs much.

5. If There Is No God, We Lose the Very Standard by Which We Critique Religions and Religious People

C. S. Lewis argued this point powerfully in *Mere Christianity* and elsewhere. Do away with God, and you have done away with transcendent meaning and power behind words like right, wrong, good, evil, justice, or injustice. Without God, you are left with contingent human tastes and opinions that, in the long run and big picture, have no more weight than we give them, and who are we anyway?

Do you see this? Who is to say that lying, adultery, and child molestation are wrong—really wrong? Sure, society might make something illegal or call it socially unacceptable—but human cultures have at various times legally or socially disapproved of everything from believing in God to believing the world revolves around the sun, from having more than one wife to refusing to take a second wife under some circumstances. Human taste, opinion, law, and culture are hardly dependable arbiters of Truth! Democracy is a fine form of government, but it makes a frightening basis for morality. Dare we think that holocausts are moral because fifty-one percent of the public votes yes? Is right determined by vote, or force, or who can shout the loudest?

Many people have arrived at the frightening conclusion made by Dostoyevsky: If there is no God, everything is permissible. Atheism leaves no standard beyond ourselves or outside ourselves to look to, to appeal to, to help us discern what is really and ultimately right and permissible, or wrong and impermissible—a powerful reason to consider alternatives.

6. If There Is No God, We Don't Make Sense

C. S. Lewis asked us in *Mere Christianity* (New York: Macmillan, 1943, p. 46) to imagine a world where eyes had never evolved:

> If the whole universe has no meaning, we should never have found out that it has no meaning—just as, if there were no light in the universe and therefore no creatures with eyes, we should never know it was dark. Dark would be without meaning. Similarly, the fact that eyes exist suggests that light must exist. And the fact that we have spiritual longings ... the fact that we even have a meaningful category of thought and speech called spirituality ... suggests that there is some corresponding reality out there which we have the capacity to "sense." That capacity would be called faith, and that reality, God.

"Just a minute," you should be saying right about now. "I don't buy that. Maybe these so-called spiritual longings are illusory. Maybe they're misguided. Maybe they're an evolutionary bug that hasn't been naturally selected out of the programming yet. Give us time, and we will evolve beyond this fluke of spirituality." And I would say, yes, maybe you're right. But I must ask you to consider how you would eliminate this spiritual longing from humanity without also eliminating the things that mean most to us when we say the word "humanity."

Francis Schaeffer, a theologian and philosopher whose writings have helped me a great deal over the years, understood this well. He told the story of a young man who had written him a letter after hearing one of his lectures. The young man said something like this: Why am I so empty? Why am I so unfulfilled? Why do I have these spiritual longings? Moss grows on the rocks in my backyard. Squirrels jump from branch to branch in the trees. The moss doesn't seem unfulfilled; the squirrels aren't plagued with questions of purpose and meaning. They are happy in their ignorance. Why do I have an insatiable thirst for a drink of something that doesn't seem to exist? Schaeffer, of course, answered him by affirming that there is indeed a reality corresponding to his thirst. His longings are not an evolutionary fluke or cruel cosmic prank, but rather evidence of an aptitude for connecting with and relating to God—who really is "there." Please don't reduce this line of thinking to a facile argument along the lines of "if I think something could exist, it must exist," which is obviously misguided. We aren't proving anything here with mathematical certainty; we are simply suggesting that if human beings have a seemingly incurable, innate, core hunger and thirst for spiritual meaning, then that is at least evidence—though certainly not proof—that there may be a reality corresponding to the desire.

Even among many who do not yet believe, there is an undeniable longing for faith, expressed by rock groups like U2 ("I still haven't found what I'm looking for") and novelists like Richard Selzer:

> My entire life has been one long search for faith. I haven't found it. I do not believe in God. Having said that,... I want you to know that I love the idea of God. I love piety. Without it, you lead your life unmoored, in a state of isolation. You are a tiny speck in a vast

universe. I am jealous, frankly. I feel as though I have missed out on the greatest thing that can happen to a person — faith in God. It must be wonderful. (*Wittenburg Door*, Summer 1989, p. 27)

There is more we could say, but the point is already clear enough: Atheism is a faith option open to you, but there are reasons to at least consider other options. This brings us to the second option. Instead of "no," some people answer the question, "Is there a God?" with this answer: I don't know. That is the topic of the next chapter.

Your Response

Choose one:

> I am an atheist because:
> I am not an atheist because:

Resources

Michael Behe's *Darwin's Black Box* details some of the reasons scientists are reconsidering the argument from design. The writings of Hugh Ross, such as *Creation and Time*, and Fred Heeren, such as *Show Me God*, further explore the relation of science and faith. And Patrick Glynn's *God: The Evidence* summarizes the decline of the secular-atheistic paradigm on several fronts. I think there is value in these works, although perhaps more for the already-convinced than for the not-yet-convinced.

I especially recommend John Polkinghorne's *The Faith of a Physicist*; Polkinghorne is both a trained scientist and an ordained Anglican priest. Equally helpful for me has been the work of John Haught, especially *God after Darwin*. And the work of Wendell Berry, especially *Life Is a Miracle*, does a great job of seeing the weaknesses in much traditional religion that is oblivious to science and in the science that claims superiority over religion. Berry's work makes believing more possible for many of us. C. S. Lewis's *Miracles* is one of the best explorations of atheism and theism I am aware of.

As for fiction, you might try Walker Percy's novels *Lancelot* and *The Last Gentleman* and its sequel, *The Second Coming*, all of which explore the question of God's existence in an entertaining, often hilarious, yet ultimately intelligent and human way.

Bruce Cockburn and David Wilcox explore faith in some extraordinarily moving and sensitive ways in their music. Cockburn's songs "Rumours of Glory," "All the Diamonds in the World," and "Broken Wheel" have been released on various albums under Columbia and Gold Castle labels. David Wilcox's "Someday Soon," "That's What the Lonely Is For," "Show the Way," "Big Mistake," and "Hold It Up to the Light" are all found on Big Horizon (A&M Records, 1994).

Prayer

I may still not be able to say I believe there is a God capable of hearing and responding to my prayers. But intellectual honesty and curiosity—and perhaps spiritual need—require me to keep the question open. If anyone is there to hear me, I want to say that I am reaching out to you; I would like to come in contact with you; I would like to explore a relationship with you. I am becoming, if not yet a believer in God, a spiritual seeker for God and for truth. Please help me.

Is "I Don't Know" Enough to Know?

This chapter explores the "I don't know" answer of agnosticism, and defines three types of agnosticism: closed agnosticism (which says, "It is impossible for anyone to know, so I reject faith of any sort"), ignosticism (which really means, "I don't care, and I choose to remain ignorant on the matter of God's existence"), and open agnosticism (which says, "I don't know" as an honest but open-minded statement expressing a lack, to date, of conclusive evidence). The chapter advocates open agnosticism over the other two.

Who Should Read This Chapter?

If you refer to yourself as an agnostic, this chapter should help you sharpen your self-understanding.

What Questions Does It Address?

What are the three types of agnosticism? Why are they all, to a degree, faith positions? What are the reasons for and against each type?

Is "I Don't Know"
Enough to Know?

"I want to believe." So reads the poster hanging prominently on the wall of Fox Mulder, of the once-popular TV show *The X Files*. Whether the poster refers to faith in extraterrestrials, faith in God, or just faith in general, I'm not sure. But it expresses the way a lot of people feel. Just the other night, a good friend of mine expressed it like this: "I don't believe in God, but I wish I could. I don't find my lack of belief comforting or helpful in the least, especially when I think about death." I asked him what obstacles kept him from believing, but he couldn't really identify anything specific. He explained, "Maybe it's not just an intellectual thing ... maybe there's a volitional element to it. Maybe I'm just not willing to believe. But I'm not an atheist; I'm not closed-minded. I guess you'd call me an agnostic."

Ask an agnostic like my friend if there is a God, and his honest answer will be "I don't know." Agnosticism is a popular option for all those who, for the reasons we considered in the previous chapter, find atheism too great a leap of faith or too extreme a solution to the problems they see in theism. Agnosticism breaks down into three types: Closed Agnosticism, Ignosticism, and Open Agnosticism. In this chapter we will try to determine which forms are more and less credible and desirable.

The term *agnosticism* itself was coined by Thomas Henry Huxley (1825–1895). His definition (from an 1889 essay,

"Agnosticism and Christianity") is fascinating in the context of our discussion here: "Agnosticism is not properly described as a negative creed, nor indeed as a creed of any kind, except insofar as it expressed absolute faith in the validity of a principle, which is as much ethical as intellectual...: that it is wrong for a man to say that he is certain of the objective truth of any proposition unless he can produce evidence which logically justifies that certainty." In the same essay, Huxley characterized — and critiqued — a well-known religious leader of his time (John Henry Cardinal Newman) with these incisive words: "... for him the attainment of faith, not the ascertainment of truth, is the highest aim of mental life." By this definition, I am eager to sign on as an agnostic. As is clear from chapter 2, like Huxley, I am careful in my use of the word "certainty," and I hope every page in this book affirms an agreement with Huxley that the ascertainment of truth is indeed the highest aim of mental life. Huxley and I would differ, of course, on our assessment of the value of faith in the pursuit of the category of truth called spiritual truth; in fact, Huxley might not even agree that such a category is valid. Many agnostics today would be closed to even the possibility that there is a category of truth for which faith would be an appropriate or necessary means of exploration. Those agnostics we could call "closed."

Closed Agnosticism

Closed agnosticism says, "It is impossible for anyone to know for certain whether there is a God or not, so I decide not to believe at all, one way or the other." In other words, the agnostic doesn't directly reject God, but he does reject faith.

The closed agnostic focuses on a key issue: the relationship between faith and knowledge (which we considered in chapter 2). Since faith is not knowledge of the type preferred by the agnostic, faith is discardable. Again, I would be quick to agree with the agnostic that many things that pass for faith are not worthy of an intelligent person's self-investment. Many things that pass for faith seem to be more make-believe than genuine belief, more self-hypnosis than perception of a reality beyond the senses, more a case of reason-minus than reason-plus, more a matter of cowering beneath understanding than soaring beyond understanding. Many things that pass for faith have more to do with brainwashing than heart-cleansing, with cultic tyranny than spiritual freedom.

But what if, given the nature of the standing of a finite creature in relation to an infinite creator, the agnostic's preferred type of knowledge is not the appropriate medium of experience? What if we are requiring light to be known through a microphone, or sound to be registered on a photovoltaic cell, or an emotion to be measurable on a bathroom scale? What if all forms of knowledge, which are appropriate for every single other entity in the universe, are in this one case inappropriate for "knowing" God—since an uncreated God would, by definition, be in a separate category from every created thing? What if, simply because God is in a category apart from every other thing or force or entity in the universe, another medium of experience is required, and what if this medium of experience involves faith of some sort? And what if this sort of faith is not an example of "bad faith" (i.e., make-believe, self-hypnosis, and so forth), and not an unwarranted claim of certainty, but rather an honest kind of good faith, worthy of the self-investment of intelligent people, an act of integrity and humility, not escape and self-deception?

In a strange way, the closed agnostic exercises a fascinating kind of faith: faith in the unprovable hypothesis that religious faith is bunk, and faith that his preferred form of rationalistic (i.e., arising from within the mind, with no outside revelation), empirical (i.e., knowable by one of the five senses) knowledge is the best or only medium to be used to know anything worth knowing in the universe—another unprovable hypothesis. I find it fascinating to look again at the words Huxley used to described agnosticism: "an absolute *faith* in the validity of a principle" (italics mine). He was aware that agnosticism itself is a kind of faith, and he was honest to admit it.

In the preceding paragraph, I used the word "hypothesis" to describe the agnostic's faith. The word deserves a closer look. As a key component in the scientific method, the hypothesis involves a hunch, an intuition, an unproven possibility that is not known, but is of sufficient interest to draw out the scientist's curiosity to do an experiment. An experiment is a quest; a journey; an often painstaking, disciplined, protracted search to test a hypothesis. Without the hypothesis, there is no motive or draw to experimentation. To reject working with hypotheses would in one way sound scientific: "I am only going to work with what is already proven by scientists of the past." But it would at the same time prove that the one making this rejection was not himself a scientist, since testing hypotheses is what scientists by definition do. Closed agnostics, then, might be comparable to people who love to read science, and believe science, and respect the findings of scientists, but who don't want to experiment themselves.

Clearly, one can be overhasty in stopping at closed agnosticism without investigating other options. Many people who may claim agnosticism, and who seem at first glance to be intellectually rigorous closed agnostics, really have committed themselves to the second option, known by the newly created term "ignosticism."

Ignosticism

Ignosticism, beneath its "I don't know" answer, means "I don't care." The ignostic agnostic says, "This subject is trivial to me. It's unimportant, not worth forming an opinion about. You might as well be asking me if I think the birds on an imaginary planet in an imaginary universe have gray or brown feathers. I don't know; I don't care; it doesn't matter. Whatever. I am happily ignorant (hence the term) about the subject."

Like closed agnosticism, ignosticism may be seen as somewhat elitist, saying something like this: "Never mind that most people through most of history, including many of the best and most brilliant in every culture, have found faith a satisfactory means for seeking God; never mind that they have felt faith was very important, worthy of sacrifice and in some cases even martyrdom. Their devotion can be dismissed as a delusion; they wasted their time and lives on something not that important."

Atheists believe that all religions are false. Agnostics (both closed agnostics and ignostics) believe that all religions are superfluous. They are making a huge faith commitment ... to the belief that the whole spiritual side of life is not worth even thinking about. If you choose ignostic agnosticism, please be aware of the magnitude of your decision, and admit that you are determining your priorities at least in part by a leap of faith. As we considered in reference to atheism, no amount of induction or deduction that I am aware of can prove that God does not exist, and given the real possibility of God's existence, deciding that the quest for God is immaterial is, at the very least, a long leap of faith.

You may have heard, in this regard, of "Pascal's Wager." Blaise Pascal, a brilliant mathematician and philosopher of the seventeenth century, put it something like this: If God exists, not seeking God must be the gravest error imaginable. If one decides to sincerely seek for God and doesn't find God, the lost effort is negligible in comparison to what is at risk by not seeking God in the first place. In other words, Pascal concluded that ignosticism is a risk too extreme for a thinking person. If there is a God, you stand to gain everything by searching for God, and you stand to lose everything by not searching. If there is no God, you stand to lose little by searching, except, perhaps, for time that could have been spent in other pursuits.

I tend to agree with Pascal, although his argument can seem flippant and superficial in some presentations. Many people obviously think Pascal was dead wrong; they are very willing to take the risk of not believing. Those people may be making a huge mistake, but if God exists, God seems to make it frighteningly easy for them to make this mistake. Or maybe it's just the ignostics themselves making it look easy.

Open Agnosticism

Some of you may feel uncomfortable with either of the two previous options. You consider yourself agnostic, but not of the closed or ignostic variety. You may be an open agnostic, who says, "God may exist, and I'm not closed to the possibility. Neither am I closed to the option of searching for God. But in all honesty, I have never had any spiritual experiences that would suggest to me that there is a God to seek, or believe in, or obey. I'm open, but sufficient evidence has not yet presented itself — or sufficient barriers to belief have not yet been removed."

Open agnostics fall along a continuum, from those who are open but not actively seeking, to those who are actively seeking. We could imagine a fifteenth-century explorer who as a child had been taught that either the world was flat or the oceans were uncrossable. Nobody had ever circumnavigated the globe, so at that point nobody could know the truth. At the moment the explorer-to-be first imagines that the world may in fact be round, or that the oceans may possibly be crossable, we could say he becomes an open agnostic — he still doesn't know, he is still not sure, but now he has doubted what he had been taught and is open to the possibility. Imagine the process that would unfold for the budding explorer as a possibility became a hunch, a hunch a belief, a belief a quest, and a quest an actual adventure. The adventure may be filled with uncertainty and error (poor Christopher Columbus, for example, thought he had reached India) — but these are necessary prices to pay for discovery.

At what point did agnosticism become faith in our analogy? I suppose it's impossible to say, just as it's impossible to answer the question "When did night give way to day this morning?" Open agnosticism is like that; it is often the dawn of faith. If I were not already a committed theist, I hope I would be an open agnostic on the seeking end of the spectrum.

As you might expect, open agnostics are very vulnerable to conversion — either to atheism, closed agnosticism, or ignosticism on the one hand, or to some embryonic form of theism on the other. If I were having a cup of coffee with an open agnostic (Joe), I would imagine a dialogue unfolding something like this:

Brian: So you're an agnostic, but you're open to the possibility of God existing.

Joe: Yes, exactly.

Brian: If God exists, would it make sense to you to pray?

Joe: Pray? I'm not sure where I'd begin.

Brian: Well, if a God is intelligent enough to create the universe, and personal enough to create conscious life, it might make sense to say, "God, are you out there?"

Joe: Kind of like ringing a doorbell to see if anybody is home, or sending a test email to see if anybody responds?

Brian: Exactly. And to take it a step farther, I could also imagine saying, "If you're there, please help me to know you."

Joe: Yeah, I wouldn't have any problem with that. It makes sense. I might feel kind of silly, like I'm talking to myself, but there wouldn't be any harm in it, I suppose, as long as we wouldn't have to take it any further than that.

Brian: My guess is that you would only take it any further than that if you wanted to, and you would only want to if your prayers were in some way answered.

Joe: It sounds like an experiment.

Brian: Yes. Faith itself is a kind of experimental process, and open agnostics are well placed to begin
experimenting.

Joe: But doesn't it then require faith to gain more
faith?

Brian: That's a great question. Do you have enough
faith to pursue more faith?

Joe: It sounds like I do.

If that is how you feel, then perhaps you are ready to move
from open agnosticism to a tentative, preliminary, experimental,
exploratory theism. Even if you aren't sure a God exists, if you
have enough faith to wonder, and even more, to ask, and even
more, to seek ... well, that's a very good start. There is a pilgrimage going on here, a spiritual quest or journey: one begins,
perhaps as an atheist or ignostic, then moves to closed agnosticism, then opens to open agnosticism, and then has the courage
to call herself or himself a spiritual seeker. This is a significant
step, a major decision. This decision faces you at this point in
our exploration, because there is little reason to continue unless
you have enough faith to continue searching. It is a yes/no matter to be worked out in your own mind and heart. "Yes" means
we are ready for the next chapter.

Your Response

Choose one:

I am a closed agnostic because:
I am an ignostic because:
I am an open agnostic because:
I am a spiritual seeker because:

Resources

There is a genre of books that we could call "Literature of Testimony," in which people tell their stories of coming to faith. One of the most famous is C. S. Lewis's *Surprised by Joy*. Another is Leo Tolstoy's *Confession*. There are hundreds more examples by figures well known (Jimmy Carter, William F. Buckley, Annie Lamott) and less known (Joni Eareckson Tada, Corrie ten Boom, Lauren Winner, Don Miller), with more being published each year. These books offer the evidence of human experience ... always subjective, but not for that reason ignorable.

There is also a genre of books giving evidences for faith called "apologetics." Hans Küng has written quite a bit in this area from a Roman Catholic perspective, as have Josh McDowell and Lee Strobel from a more Protestant perspective. Again, C. S. Lewis is hard to beat, having come to faith through real intellectual struggle himself; see *Mere Christianity*. Billy Graham's writings shouldn't be forgotten; although very simple, they are also very clear and have helped many people. Speaking of which, N. T. Wright's *Simply Christian* is both simple and intelligent. Peter Kreeft's *Yes or No: Straight Answers to Tough Questions about Christianity* offers a very readable and reasonable exploration of common questions. I highly recommend it.

Prayer

God, I want to grow in faith. I don't want to remain stagnant or slip backward. I want to develop a faith that enriches my life, overflows to my neighbors, and in some significant way adds something positive to the world. Through this, I want my life to honor you. Help me, when difficulties come, not to give up, let go, or turn back. Help me be like a child, learning and growing, resilient and energetic, all the days of my life.

If There Is One God, Why Are There So Many Religions?

This chapter considers the third answer — yes — to the question, "Is there a God?" It suggests that the welter of religious options can be simplified to four: pantheism, polytheism, dualism, and monotheism. It briefly describes each, and suggests that pantheism and monotheism are the two main alternatives for people today. While acknowledging value in each option, the author recommends monotheism, and then describes "good-faith monotheism."

Who Should Read This Chapter?

This is one of the more important chapters in the book for people who are not already convinced regarding monotheism.

What Questions Does It Address?

What are the four main options within theism? What can pantheism and monotheism learn from one another? Why does the author think "bad monotheism" is the worst enemy of "good monotheism," and what does he mean by these terms?

If There Is One God, Why Are There So Many Religions?

When you are just starting to search for God, it can be bewildering, overwhelming, just trying to figure out where to begin. Which version or model of God do you pursue? There seem to be so many out there!

It can feel like shopping. I speak as one who does not love to shop. (That sentence qualifies as one of the year's greater understatements.) When I need something, my motto is "Get in, select, pay, get out"—as fast as I would if I were venturing through a swarm of thirsty mosquitoes. When I need to buy a car in the next year or so, I want to give my savings to my brother, and say, "Hey, Pete, will you go pick the best car for me?" That makes sense because there are so many makes and models, so many accessories and options. I feel completely unqualified to make a choice, and I am paralyzed by the range of options. Pete, however, is much more knowledgeable than I, and I trust him. Shopping—especially for a major purchase like a car—is an ordeal I would rather avoid.

A car can be mine if I pay for it, even if someone else searches for it. Not so, I would think, with a spiritual quest. No one can choose faith for another person, so it looks as if each of us has to venture into the megamall of religions to try to find the one that is right for us. That sounds depressing to a non-shopper like me!

The good news is that the situation isn't as complex as you might think. There are four basic "models" of God, and two of them stand out as more worthy of further investigation. Here are the four basic models:

1. God is everything. The universe itself is God. God is the whole, the sum of all the parts. This model is called pantheism.
2. There are many gods. No single one of them is supreme. This option is called polytheism.
3. There are two Gods, one good or creative, one evil or destructive. They are caught in an eternal struggle, perhaps like the positive and negative charges in electricity. This model is called dualism.
4. There is one God. This God is good, supreme, and creative. This option is called monotheism.

Of course, you can imagine some other options too — monotheism with a God who is, for example, evil, powerless, apathetic, or uncaring — or dualism where both Gods are evil, and so forth. But for a variety of reasons, no one has ever decided to believe any of these options, at least not for very long, or with sufficient passion to convince many other people to believe similarly.

In your quest for God, then, you have these four options. Let's begin with the middle options, since they are rarely believed these days, and relatively easy to dismiss.

Polytheism

Polytheism, followed by a wide array of people from the ancient Greeks and Romans to primitive tribespeople to some modern-day Wiccans and New Agers, asserts that the universe is peopled (or godded) by numerous deities. Among primitives, perhaps trees and animals were seen to have spirits, or one's ancestors were believed to have entered the realm of the gods—and as such should be revered.

Some practitioners of witchcraft and New Age who speak of many deities shouldn't always be taken literally when they speak this way. What they call gods may actually mean to them concepts, or myths, which they do not believe to have actual reality outside of their own imagination or psyche, or perhaps the collective psyche of a culture. people often speak of having "demons" in this way, not asserting a belief in devilish spirits, but in dark and ugly sides of their own psyche. (Of course, many other people believe in actual demons too.) People who speak in this metaphorical way about gods or deities may in fact be atheists or agnostics incognito, or they could be pantheists, dualists, or monotheists too.

Bona fide polytheists exist, but they are quite rare, especially among educated people. (If you are wondering about Hinduism, which may appear polytheistic on one level, its many gods are actually believed to be manifestations or emanations of one ultimate divine reality, which we will shortly consider under the category of pantheism.) Why? For one thing, polytheism seems to raise more questions than it answers. For example, if there are many gods, might not one of them be supreme, the originator of the others, or might there be an even greater being behind these beings, that "God farther back" being the only real entity worthy of the name God?

Dualism

Also uncommon are dualists, believing that there are two opposite, eternal, ultimate deities. This should not be confused with the more typical monotheistic belief in God and Satan; clearly, in that scenario God is ultimate and supreme, and Satan a created (and later deformed) being. Neither should it be confused with the somewhat similar "Star Wars" vision of "the Force," which is good and creative, with a "Dark Side" split off from it, which is evil and destructive. Rather, true dualism sees two eternal, parallel forces, neither of which is "higher" than or prior to the other, both of which are equally ultimate.

In history, dualism behaves like an unstable chemical compound. It wants to resolve in one of two directions—either toward pantheism (where the two entities actually comprise one larger, ultimate entity) or monotheism (where one entity is ultimate and the other, contingent).

And thus our quest moves toward this tentative conclusion: There appears to be a God, most likely either of the pan- or mono- variety. Both varieties deserve our serious consideration. Perhaps there is truth to be found in both? Yet they differ significantly....

Pan- or Mono- **Differences?**

On a macro level, pantheism says that everything is God. Monotheism says that everything was created by God. Pantheism says that if you subtract the universe—all its matter, all its energy, all its spirit—you have subtracted God. Monotheism says that if you subtract the universe, God has not been diminished one iota. Pantheism suggests that you and I are part of God, that we are, in fact, God. Monotheism suggests that you and I have a distinct existence as creations of God, and as such are capable of relationship with God. Pantheism emphasizes the fundamental unity of all things including God. Monotheism celebrates the unity of God and the diversity of all things, along with the possibility of a relationship in which they come together.

Pantheism

Pantheism has much that attracts a thinking person. First, in our divided and polarizing world, we seem to need some centripetal force to counterbalance the centrifugal forces that thrust us apart — hence a certain attraction for pantheism's emphasis on the unity of all things. Second, pantheism not only elevates humanity to the level of divinity; it also elevates all of nature — every bird, every tree, every rock, every drop of water and grain of sand equally sharing the status of being part of God. In our world where neighbor fails to respect neighbor, and where humanity fails to respect the environment, this elevation seems healthy, restorative, therapeutic. Third, pantheism easily explains the experience we all (I hope) have from time to time — when watching a sunset, pondering a flower or tree, touching a whale, observing a baby's birth, making love, grieving a death — the feeling that what we experience is holy, sacred, precious. The pantheist might say, "Of course: All is God. Your experience is simply God awakening to the experience of Itself."

But pantheism has some rather troubling implications. If distinctions are lost in ultimate oneness, and if humanity is part of the deity, then rapist and rape victim, murderer and murdered, child molester and molestee, oppressive dictator and despised minority are equally expressions of the One. The cost of avoiding divisions turns out to be the distinction between good and evil. Both are comprised in the One. Whatever is, is … and it is the One; it is God. There is no space "outside" God for evil to be planned and enacted and even celebrated; the whole grim process of evil, then, must take place within God.

If you believe that is the best model to fit the universe and your experience in it, then you may decide to become a pantheist. But please be realistic, and face the full logical implications of pantheism before you sign on. Take it as it is, or don't take it at all.

You might be tempted to try to "fix" pantheism, to domesticate the implications of saying that good and evil are illusory categories, that both are part of God. You might say, for example, that God/the universe itself is evolving toward something better (through, for example, a process of karma where justice is served through life experience, where bad actions bring bad consequences, leading to gradual self-correction within "the system"). You might say that good is triumphing and evil is being purified like dross from gold ore, that truth is overcoming and misperceptions are being exposed and eradicated like darkness by light. But when you say these things, at that same moment, you are acknowledging a higher principle of goodness behind the universe, a preexisting standard of good to which the universe is being conformed, a universal code or conscience by which goodness and evil, truth and error, wisdom and folly are distinguished. And the more important to you that this preexisting standard of goodness behind the universe becomes, the more you start sounding like a monotheist rather than a pantheist. Soon, you start thinking that the standard or conscience or principle behind the universe is greater than the universe itself and is distinct from it and independent of it and prior to it: voilà, a singular supreme entity ... which sounds a lot like monotheism to me.

As you can see, as attractive as pantheism seems, and as superior as it appears when compared with atheism, agnosticism, polytheism, or dualism, I find myself drawn beyond pantheism to monotheism. Pantheism certainly has much to offer, and our understanding of monotheism is enriched, I believe, by dialogue with monotheism's primary theological colleague. Incidentally, if Christian monotheism is true, pantheism might not be so much false as it is "not true yet," for Christians believe that history is flowing toward a goal in which God is in everything, and everything is in God (see, for example, Ephesians 1:10, 22–23; 4:6, 10). Some people use the term *panentheism* to describe this pantheism-and-monotheism-in-dialogue.

My honest sense in my own search is that logic drives me behind the many, behind the two, behind the all, to one God "over all, through all, and in all."

I see a dynamic tension between pantheism and monotheism. Just as the pantheist can, in my opinion, go astray by coupling good and evil within God, so the monotheist can go astray by completely uncoupling God and the universe, acting as if there is no relationship between the two. Just as I believe the pantheist has much to learn from the monotheist, so I believe the monotheist can benefit from dialogue with the pantheist.

Monotheism

As the pantheist could readily point out, monotheism has apparent downsides too. For example, as soon as we say there is one God, the natural question arises: Which one? As soon as we ask that question, aren't we inevitably setting ourselves up for Crusades, holy wars, jihads, division, controversy, bigotry, confusion, contradiction, overwhelming complexity?

Aren't we right back to where we started—with an impossibly complex "shopping" task? Aren't the very complexity and strife unleashed by monotheism the turnoffs that lead many people on to pantheism—or to atheism or agnosticism? Is there any way to accept monotheism without falling into endless controversy? At the end of our search, will we find ourselves preaching frantic damnation on street corners to passersby, because they don't believe in the same one God we do?

The path ahead, I think, requires us to pursue monotheism—but to do so carefully and to acknowledge that monotheism itself, like faith, can take many forms, good and bad. As I see it, good monotheism's greatest enemy isn't pantheism or even atheism or agnosticism, but rather bad monotheism. What would constitute good monotheism? Here are three of my own opinions on that question.

1. Good Monotheism Makes for Peace

Let's say we monotheists differ with the pantheists by saying that the universe is not identifiable as God; but let's say we agree that the universe in many wonderful ways reflects God, just as a painting reflects the artist, a song the musician, a poem the poet, a novel the writer, or a child the parent. (Actually, the ways in which God is seen in the universe must be even more wonderful and immediate than these analogies. More on this in a minute.) In this way, although we can't exactly say that when we see all things we see God, we can say that in or through all things we can see some beautiful reflection of or fascinating clues about God. (In the case of evil things, we see something about God by contrast, or by conspicuous absence.)

If the universe is full of reflections of God in this way, then as monotheists, we would expect every religion to have caught some glimpses of God's glory, being surrounded, as we all are, by the beauty of God reflected in creation. That means that we can begin, instead of with quarrels, with dialogue, listening and sharing with members of each religion, affirming all the common ground we find we share—not, as the pantheist would say, because all things are God, but because all things created by God reflect their creator, and thus the universe is riddled with what songwriter Bruce Cockburn calls "rumours of glory." That means we can look for, and affirm, the points where each religion and individual have caught on to the rumors and recognized the clues. We can be irenic, not combative, and respectful, not insulting.

2. Good Monotheism Affirms God's Connection with the Universe

The very word religion offers insight in this regard. The prefix "re-" means "again," and the root "lig" (as in ligament) means "connect." Religion, then, is about the reconnection of the creator with creation; it is about reconnecting people with God, people with one another. The human predicament, monotheists believe, is that disconnect is possible, and not just possible, that it is actual, that it has happened. We intelligent creations have the capacity to at least partially disconnect from God via willful rebellion, defiance, resistance, indifference, or ignorance—and we have used that capacity with tragic results. When we disconnect from God, we find ourselves becoming internally disconnected, "dis-integrated," hence experiencing shame and fear and duplicity and hypocrisy. Our disconnect from God and ourselves leads inevitably to further fragmentation, disconnection from other people, disconnection from our environment.

If our disconnection from God creates our own human predicament, it also creates a dilemma for God, if we can speak in such terms. Put crudely, God has a problem.

A. If, on the one hand, God allows our disconnection in the name of freedom ("They shouldn't be forced to obey; they shouldn't be forced to worship; love cannot by definition be forced. They made their bed; let them lie in it. Let their choices stand."), then we plunge toward destruction. Like branches disconnected from the tree, without God we will wither and die. These questions naturally arise: "Doesn't God care? Would it even be responsible of a creator to make creatures capable of such self-destruction, and then provide no way of escape for them if they chose the bitter path?"

B. If, on the other hand, God interferes excessively with our disconnection in the name of love ("I can't let them destroy themselves and each other. I care too much for them to allow that.") or justice ("No one will defy my just will."), then do we become robots, puppets, rats in a behavioral conditioning experiment? These questions naturally arise: "Doesn't God respect our dignity and freedom? What does it prove if God forces us to comply?"

This divine-human dilemma is resolved easily by two forms of monotheism:

A. Determinism resolves it by saying that, yes, people are hopelessly disconnected from God, and that, yes, God cares for some and shows it by forgiving them and reconnecting them. (Natural questions: "Why some and not others? Why not everyone?" To which honest determinists say, "We don't know.")

B. Universalism resolves it by saying that, yes, people are hopelessly disconnected from God, and that, yes, God cares for everyone and shows it by reconnecting everyone. (Natural questions: "What difference does it make if a person is good or bad then? Hitler and Mother Teresa receive the same treatment? People are reconciled with God whether they like it or not, even against their will?" To which honest universalists say, "We haven't figured that all out yet.")

Other monotheists don't see an easy resolution here and are content (or maybe not content, but at least resigned) to leave the dilemma to be just that, seeing its resolution as a mystery ... for now at least. Like the others, they say, "We don't know; we haven't figured that all out yet," although they make this admission earlier along than the others. In spite of these differences, all of these monotheists agree on this: God cares about the universe and doesn't want to let it disconnect, wither, and die, and God is involved in the unfolding of a dramatic story of reconnection, a story we all find ourselves in the middle of. Our "re-connecting" is what "re-ligion" is all about.

3. Good Monotheism Emphasizes the Role of Creation in Revealing God

Good monotheism (unlike the "industrial-strength monotheism" too common in recent centuries) does not allow the distinction between creator and creation to so devalue creation as to make creation little more than a utilitarian resource. Far from it!

Let me illustrate it in this way. I live near Washington, DC, which has many beautiful art galleries. In the National Gallery hangs a beautiful painting by Rembrandt. It is one of the paintings into which the artist painted his own face. Art lovers feel a reverence for the painting; you can sense it when they enter that room of the gallery. (In fact, it is often their reverence for the painting that leads them to learn more about the artist and develop a reverence for the artist.) There is a hush, a concentration, a thrill, a wonder. Similarly (as we will see in more detail in a later chapter), healthy monotheists feel a reverence for all that exists. (There are important ecological implications here, aren't there?)

Art Gallery

We find ourselves living in an art gallery: Every goldfinch and osprey, each trout and barracuda, all Appaloosas and elephants, all mica and magma, each woodland fern and live oak, every red raspberry and green tomato, even all hydrogen and oxygen ... are unique masterpieces, amazing wonders. And not only can we enjoy the art, but we can also know the Artist, relate to the Artist, tell the Artist about our feelings of gratitude, wonder, and awe. And not only that ... we can conceive of ourselves as artwork in process, as part of an awesome, unfolding master-creation in progress.

And more: All of creation thus reveals the Artist. We are surrounded not only by beauty that inspires, but beauty that teaches. The Christian doctrine of the Holy Spirit and the Jewish concept of the Wisdom of God both support this view, suggesting that God speaks, teaches, and enlightens through all of life. Jesus' use of parables similarly would reinforce this view. For his disciples, there was no classroom but the field, the dirt road, the cottage, the mountainside: All of life was the classroom, full of vehicles for enlightenment. Christian monotheists like me, in fact, have a special reason to see a strong linkage between the creator and the creation; we believe that God actually did paint himself into the picture, thus honoring and ennobling the picture to an astounding degree, showing profound solidarity between creator and creation. Not everyone sees it this way, of course. At any rate, our next step is to deal with some problems with monotheism, as I am describing it, that may already have begun to bother you.

Your Response

I am attracted to the following model in my spiritual search:

> Pantheism, because ...
> Polytheism, because ...
> Dualism, because ...
> Monotheism, because ...

I affirm the following characteristics of "good monotheism":

> Makes for peace
> Affirms God's connection with the universe
> Emphasizes the role of creation in revealing God
> Other

Resources

C. S. Lewis's *Mere Christianity* makes a strong case for monotheism. Marcus Borg's *The Heart of Christianity*, N. T. Wright's

Simply Christian, and my *A Generous Orthodoxy* all attempt to present Christian monotheism in accessible ways.

For information on world religions and their views of God, one of the best guides is Huston Smith, *The World's Religions*.

Prayer

God, I may have sufficient faith to believe you exist (although I may still have doubts at times), but I need increased understanding of which approach to you is best, for me at least. Should you be understood more as the sum total of everything, as pantheism suggests, or as the Supreme Being who created the sum total of everything, as monotheism suggests? I ask for guidance and enlightenment in this regard. Help my pursuit of you to be a "good faith" pursuit. Although I am thinking hard and searching for you sincerely, I am also aware that without help from beyond myself, my efforts have little or no chance of succeeding. Please help me.

The fact that I am praying suggests that, though I can't claim to understand fully or to be free of doubts and questions, I indeed have some degree of faith that you are a personal God who is capable of a relationship with me, one of your creatures. If I didn't believe this to some degree, I wouldn't be talking to you at all.

Do You Seriously Expect Me to Think of God As an Old Man with a Long White Beard?

This chapter addresses a number of common objections or frustrations that people have with monotheism, regarding God's personality, gender, subtlety, and the like.

Who Should Read This Chapter?

If you feel that monotheism as it is usually presented is somewhat beneath you, that it seems backward or outmoded or just doesn't make sense, this chapter may help you. If you are one of the already-convinced, this chapter should help you better understand and help others who have these objections.

What Questions Does It Address?

In what way can we speak of God being personal and relational without making God sound like a "big old guy in the sky"? What is deism, and why is it attractive? How can we understand and deal with the apparent chauvinism involved in referring to God as "he"? Why isn't God more obvious?

Do You Seriously Expect Me to Think of God As an Old Man with a Long White Beard?

In this chapter, we need to clean up some messes that we may have inadvertently created in our dialogue so far.

We began a previous chapter with the question "What is God?"—and we never really answered it. The question has a certain charming naïveté when you think about it. Who do we think we are—we small creatures with three-pound brains, a few limited senses, and life spans barely long enough to get to know our neighborhood, much less the planet, and much less the galaxy, and much less the universe, and much less still its creator! Who do we think we are to be able to define or even describe the creator of DNA, galaxies, dust mites, blue whales, the carbon cycle, light, and a billion other realities we have no notion about whatsoever, no awareness of at all?

Yet even given our limitations, perhaps some real degree of knowledge is possible. Consider this analogy to my children. Imagine them when they were younger, say under eight. If you had asked them, "Who is your dad?" how would they have answered? They couldn't have told you about my height, weight, temperature, blood pressure, heart rate, or any other vital statistics. They were incapable of saying anything intelligent about my genetic makeup. They didn't know much about my philosophy of life, what books I had read, what places I had visited, which degrees I had earned, what music I liked, how many languages I spoke. They certainly didn't comprehend my sexuality or my financial position, nor could they identify with many of my adult emotions—including the depth of my love for them. My doctors, teachers, and colleagues knew more about me, in these senses, than they did.

Yet in another sense, they knew me intimately, in a way beyond anyone else. They knew the smell of my skin, the feel of my hair (which I still had back then), the strength of my hands, the fine nuances of my smile. And more—was I faithful or inconstant, generous or stingy, forgiving or hard, playful or grim, kind or cruel? And even more—who was I *to them*? Who could know these things better than they? True, their limitations as children gave them certain disadvantages in understanding their father, but their relationship as my children gave them other incomparable advantages.

The Relational Advantage

So we are not a group of fish trying to learn about camels—to which we have no relation and next to nothing in common; we are fish trying to learn about the water and currents in which we live and move. We are not birds studying the distances between two stars in a distant galaxy—places inaccessible and irrelevant to us; we are birds exploring the wind and air that surround us. We are not scholars researching an ancient Chinese emperor—a matter of objectivity and disinterestedness; we are sons and daughters who want to get to know our father—someone with whom we have an essential relationship. We are creations in the universe God created and to which God is somehow present—we are part of God's universe, and God is therefore part of ours, and in that way, we are inseparably related.

But as soon as we start speaking in these familiar terms, comparing God to a father, we must address three issues we will need to deal with sooner or later—and it might as well be sooner. First, aren't we making a huge leap to speak of God as personal (he or she) to begin with—rather than as impersonal (it)? Second, even if God is personal, what reasons do we have to believe that God is relational—that a big, transcendent God would want to be involved in our puny, pedestrian lives? And third, why speak of God as male, as father—why not as female, as mother?

1. Personal or Impersonal?

Many people resist the idea of a living, personal God, and with good reason. When they think of a person, they think of rather quaint but silly images—such as God as a Santa-esque old man with a long white beard ... or as an immature tyrant prone to throwing temper tantrums ... or as a forgetful manager who needs constant reminders (via prayer) lest he forget important details in his universe ... or as an absentminded professor who naively started this experiment called the universe that since has gone more than slightly out of control.

Our problem in this regard is probably a matter of words—perhaps confusing "personal" with "human." To illustrate, think of the following items: gravity, helium, water, coal, a fern, a frog, a parrot, a golden retriever, a chimpanzee, a human being. The first three bring us from energy to matter, from gas to solid, and from invisible to visible. When we get to the fern, we move from nonliving to living. From fern to frog, we cross the boundary to animate. I don't know any frogs very well, but with my limited exposure, they seem to have a little, but not much, in the way of personality. Parrots have more, and golden retrievers and chimpanzees more still ... and human beings, more still. Now, with each step up the ladder, we didn't lose the qualities of the previous steps; rather, we added more capabilities, more depth ... while we subtracted previous limitations, going from energy to matter to form to solidity to plant life to animal life to warm-blooded life to mammalian life to primate life to human life.

Let's imagine we inserted a million rungs in our ladder after human beings, each rung suggesting more developed, less limited beings, with personalities as far beyond our own as ours are beyond a bullfrog's—not less developed with each ascending rung, but more. And we could insert another million, and another, and we would be getting some idea of the way in which we can speak of God being living and personal.

Of course, I am not asking you to believe that God is living and personal to the same small degree and with the same limitations we are. I am not saying that God inhales and exhales, digests and ages, sleeps and wakes. Rather, I am suggesting that God is living and personal not in a way less than us, but more. And I am suggesting that the fact that we share these qualities called life and personality means there is a bridge, a connecting point, a common language, a medium of communication. It means that both we and God come equipped with a telephone link or wireless modem so we can interface. Obviously, one party's potentials dwarf the other party's, but nevertheless, connectivity is possible. That's a pretty wonderful thought.

It is illogical to think otherwise, really. A creator can't create beings greater than himself. The fact that living personalities (humans, chimps, golden retrievers) exist in the universe demands that the creator must not be below life and personality—but instead must be, in the truest sense, the Life and Personality that all living creations in some small way reflect. Now I know many people who don't like to speak this way. They prefer to speak of God as a force or perhaps a principle, and I think they do so to avoid confusing themselves with the kinds of silly human notions we mentioned earlier (Santa Claus, petty tyrant, forgetful manager, and so forth). If by "force" we mean something mysterious, powerful, and beyond our power to fully comprehend, we are speaking accurately. If by "principle" we mean something true in and of itself, requiring no proof or argument, again, I think we are speaking accurately. But if by force or principle, we mean something nonliving and nonpersonal, something on a lower rung than many creations including ourselves and golden retrievers and ferns, then, again, I think we are imagining an absurdity. I think you will agree.

2. Personal But Nonrelational?

Many people will grant that God could not be less than personal, but they argue, "Don't you think the Creator of the Universe has bigger fish to fry than answering the prayers of elementary-school children and old women?" The objection has some merit, but not much, as illustrated by the following counter-objections:

A. What's wrong with elementary-school children and old women?

B. Actually, I can't think of the Creator having any fish to fry at all—i.e., problems to solve. Furthermore, I can't think of anything more important—or interesting, for that matter—than an elementary-school child or old woman. Who do you expect would deserve more of God's attention—lawyers or politicians?

C. You don't think that God has limited energy and strength, do you—that God works up such a sweat keeping galaxies spinning and black holes swallowing ("big fish to fry") that God doesn't have enough time (enough time? with God?) or energy or concentration left to pay attention to this little planet or individual people on it?

D. You haven't fallen into the "big is important" fallacy, have you—that physical size somehow corresponds to actual importance?

E. You don't think that God lacks mental ability, do you—that God's eyes (so to speak) don't focus down to details such as sparrows, kids, grandmothers?

Of course, in these wisecrack retorts I risk not taking this question seriously enough. And I would be making a mistake to do so, because deism—the belief in a personal but distant, uninvolved creator—is a belief I respect, held by many people (past and present) whom I also respect. Deism, like a lot of movements, makes more sense when you see what it was against, in historical context. To do that, imagine a pair of sensitive, intelligent people in the eighteenth century having a beer in an American pub ...

Frank: Did you hear about the latest war?

Jeff: Where now? Every time you turn around, there's another war.

Frank: Sad but true. This one's in Flogistan.

Jeff: Don't tell me: religion's behind it. Those Flogistanis are a religious lot.

Frank: Of course. What else could it be? One party believes that cleanliness is next to godliness, and they've passed laws requiring everyone to bathe at least annually.

Jeff: Don't tell me — the other party believes that man's natural aroma is God-given, and therefore shouldn't be eradicated by soap or covered by cologne.

Frank: Exactly! How did you know? The Cleanliness Party killed two hundred ... after torturing them in God's name by making them eat soap. The Natural Aroma Party retaliated by spreading human excrement through the capital city, also in the name of God. Dozens have died because of disease; a plague has broken out. Not only that: full-scale civil war has erupted, each side claiming it is God's army, inflicting his wrath on the other side.

Jeff: A real curse, this religion business, always causing wars, death, division, killing. Wouldn't it be nice if we could conduct our lives free of religion. Imagine there's no heaven ...

Frank: Yes, but we need God as the Creator and sustainer of moral law. If there is no God, then everything is permissible.

Jeff: Good point. Let's postulate that the deity exists and should be honored as the giver of life, liberty, moral law, and reason. And let's postulate that the deity wishes us to use our reason to solve our problems, without bringing him into it.

Frank: Brilliant! Such a belief will lead to the elevation of human beings instead of their constant descent into petty and pathetic religious squabbles which, in spite of their triviality, are all turned into God-sized Major Issues. To promote this new concept, the deity should be conceived of in the most high-tech imagery possible ... how about as a Clockmaker? He designed and created the clock of our universe, wound it up, set it in motion, and has no need or desire to interfere or intervene. It is our responsibility to ... act responsibly, under God.

Jeff: I think we have something here, my friend. Let me buy you another drink ...

I can imagine, if I were drinking nearby and overheard their conversation, being the first one to sign on as a deist. Aren't they right to be outraged at the atrocities and trivialities committed in God's name by various petty religions? I never cease to be amazed at the ridiculous trivialities we believers can focus on and fight about.

Deism made sense in its day as a reaction against religious wrangling and warfare. But reactionary movements often lack lasting stability and staying power, and deism is a case in point. Today, deism tends to be a stopover on the flight, not a final destination. People (or families) moving from faith to agnosticism or atheism, or the reverse, often stop there for a while (or a generation). Deism, as I see it, was against something worth being against, but in the process became for something not worth being for: a distant, uninvolved God whose personal care for individuals is severely limited. This is yet another case of bad monotheism (here, constant religious bickering) being good monotheism's worst enemy. We should be grateful for deism's attempt to remedy the situation, and learn from deism (with its emphasis, for example, on human responsibility, and its sense of proportion — not making God the arbiter of trivialities or the justifier of pettiness), without limiting ourselves to deism's severely limited, uninvolved deity.

Although few people would call themselves deists today, the term probably fits a good many people, including those who say they believe in God as a Life Force of some sort, but not a personal, relational God. As I have said, I think many people have moved in this direction for understandable and commendable reasons (avoiding the cantankerous spirit of bad monotheism). But I must mention one less commendable reason. Deism can be attractive as a low-cost, convenient religious option ... low cost and convenience being fine qualifications for choosing a bank, perhaps, but questionable for choosing a focus for one's faith. As C. S. Lewis aptly said in *Mere Christianity*, this form of deism

> gives one much of the emotional comfort of believing in God and none of the less pleasant consequences....
>
> When you are feeling fit and the sun is shining and you do not want to believe that the whole universe is a mere mechanical dance of atoms, it is nice to be able to think of this great mysterious Force rolling on through the centuries and carrying you on its crest. If, on the

other hand, you want to do something rather shabby, the Life-Force, being only a blind force, with no morals and no mind, will never interfere with you like that troublesome God we learned about when we were children. The Life-Force is a sort of tame God. You can switch it on when you want, but it will not bother you. All the thrills of religion and none of the cost.

There are other ways to deal with the cantankerous spirit of bad monotheism, as we will see. The deists, it seems to me, were right—a Supreme Being wouldn't be about fueling petty party feuds; but neither, I think, would a Supreme Being refuse to come close to us, get involved with us, allow us to come into relationship with him. What do you think?

3. Male or Female?

The fact that I just used the word "him" for God in the previous sentence brings us to the problem of gender. This is largely (but not totally) a problem of some languages, such as English. (In many languages, I understand, this problem hardly exists because their pronouns aren't gender-specific.) Consider these facts about the English language: (1) In English, we can speak of an inanimate genderless thing (stone, table, dirt), but not an inanimate male or female thing (such as a ?—we can't even identify such a thing!). Why? Because in English gender is only a characteristic of living things. (We might as well speak of a solid gas or a poisonous nutrient, since a gendered inanimate object is to us equally an absurdity.) This situation is quite different in the Romance languages, for example, where everything has gender. (2) Of course, in English, we do sometimes ascribe personality (and along with it, gender) to an inanimate thing—like a ship, for instance, calling it "she"—but when we do, we only ascribe gender after we have personified the object. (3) Conversely, in English, when we speak of living things, we have the opposite problem; the more personal they are, the less we speak of them without assigning them a gender. If we don't, we seem to call their personality into question. For example, we have no problem calling a worm (a creature seemingly low on personality, agreed?) an "it"—but we refer to our golden retrievers as "he" or "she." Regarding humans, we feel uncomfortable calling a baby of unknown gender an "it" for very long; we need to know if "it" is really a "he" or "she."

So, we seem bound by the rules of our language to ascribe gender to God to express our recognition of God as a personal being. But consider this: If God is not bound by human personality as we know it, then surely God is not bound by gender as we know it either. If that's the case, to call God "he" or "she" would mean "he + she + ." In other words, God is not less than male or female, but neither is God equal to male or female in human terms: Just as God does with our categories of personhood, surely God must include and transcend our gender categories as well.

Beyond Semantics

But here is where our problem moves beyond the semantic to the practical. Along with our language limitations, through the centuries we humans have had—and still have—some very restrictive views on the females of our species (please excuse me for stating the obvious). These restrictive views have varied from culture to culture, finding expression in everything from forced female circumcision to excluding women from democratic processes, from considering them as uneducable to counting them as property.

And no doubt, wherever languages like English lead people to refer to God with masculine pronouns, there has been the temptation to assume that God is actually masculine ... thus implying that man is more godlike, and woman less so—and thus justifying and perhaps even encouraging all kinds of oppression and subjugation and mistreatment of women. To remedy this situation, some have tried to balance "he" and "she" references to God (an option I don't prefer for a number of reasons that would take us even further on a tangent to discuss). Others have tried to avoid using pronouns for God altogether (an option I prefer when stylistically appropriate). Still others have hoped that by capitalizing the first letter (e.g., "He" or "Him"), they would be showing that God has a category of His (or God's?) own ... thus transcending the merely human categories of gender; and others still continue to use standard English practice with masculine pronouns, keeping in mind their belief that God is not a male.

As you have probably noticed, I follow the second practice whenever I can. It isn't a neat solution, but I don't see a perfect solution, given the limits of human language and, in our case, the human language called English. Perhaps this challenge goes along with the challenge of faith: Just as faith forces us to deal with realities that exceed our understanding, so it challenges us to deal with realities that stretch our normal language and prove it less than fully adequate. (This is, of course, as we would expect. After all, Whom are we talking about?)

Maternal Imagery?

Having addressed the language problem, though, this digression will not be complete until we go beyond language and deal with the issue of imagery. If God is not limited to he-ness, would not maternal imagery be as effective as paternal? And we can quickly say, "Yes. It's only logical." The Bible itself uses maternal imagery for God on a number of occasions (see Isaiah 42:14; Luke 15:8 – 10; or Psalm 17:8, for example.) And it asserts in its opening chapters that male and female together reflected God's image. In modern times, after viewing a movie like *The Spitfire Grill* or *Lorenzo's Oil* or *Tsotsi*, or throughout history everywhere, after observing the real-life love and dedication and sacrifice of mothers, can anyone doubt that one gets beautiful and brilliant glimpses of God in the quiet heroism of mothers?

Why, then, do paternal images seem to dominate, especially in the teachings of Jesus? Why are there so few maternal images of God in the Bible?

Our search for answers could explore any number of possibilities. For example, the Bible was originally written by and for people of patriarchal cultures; in that context, paternal imagery would be the highest and most honoring imagery available for God, whereas maternal imagery could imply an insult or lesser honor. In fact, in those cultures, advanced age (which may have begun at forty or fifty!) was also revered: As a result — imagery of God as an old man with a white beard, which seems quaint or even silly to us, was an attempt to relate God to the most respected, venerated model available to their imagination.

In addition, maternal imagery was common for territorial deities in the ancient world. In fact, in many cultures, goddesses were prevalent and gods were few. Goddess imagery was often highly sexualized and "celebrated" via temple prostitution and orgiastic cultic practices — more reasons for the biblical writers to avoid it. Also, people of the ancient world generally held the "garden model" of femininity: The seed of life was carried by the man, with the woman's womb serving as the garden in which the seed could be planted. It was the man, therefore, who carried the vital function, with the woman being in the passive receiver role—far different from our more egalitarian (and genetically accurate) views of conception and gestation today. In that context, only paternal imagery would do justice to the vitality and vigor of God.

Today, we would feel much freer to use maternal imagery than the ancients. In doing so, of course, we would want to be careful to avoid stereotyping women (inferring, for example, that they only reflect the tenderness and gentleness and emotional side of God, ignoring their strength and bravery and intelligence) and excessively sexualizing God (an underrated danger we may still be somewhat oblivious to, content as we often are to see God in excessively or exclusively masculine terms). If some overmasculinize their image of God (according to dominating, war-like, or hot-tempered stereotypes), we aren't helping ourselves and our children to swing to the opposite extreme by overfeminizing God (according to some list of contrasting stereotypes), and neither are we helping the situation by trying to "neuter" God, I would imagine (a rather horrific thought). God, in whose image male and female were created, must include all authentically masculine and feminine qualities and at the same time transcend them.

Why Isn't God More Obvious?

This discussion of gender is a small piece of a much larger conversation we could have about the different metaphors we use for God. But casting a shadow over our exploration of these metaphors is a larger question: Why do we need metaphors at all? Why isn't God more obvious? We don't need to talk about finding ways to experience, say, sunlight or rain or tiredness or gravity ... our experience of these things is unmediated. You can't help but experience them because they're so real, so common. Why isn't God as obvious and unavoidable as rain or gravity?

The "problem" could lie with God. This problem could simply be evidence that God doesn't exist, or that if God exists, God simply wants to be left alone and have us get on with our lives and civilization without reference to God. Or there's another option: perhaps God has reasons for not wanting to be obvious. I can think of an analogy from the church where I served as pastor for over twenty years. We had an internet discussion group, where people could post messages and raise questions and offer answers. It was a great place for intelligent discourse and educational dialogue. As pastor, though, I tried to be a silent participant. If I were to give too many answers in too many postings, others would be tempted to pull back ... my presence would intimidate them. The discussion group would stop being a community dialogue, and would become a one-way monologue, with people asking questions and "Mr. Know-It-All" answering. Since my goal was for them to develop through interaction (not for me to show off how much I knew), I chose to stay in the background, seldom posting a message of my own.

Or to return to a paternal image, as a father I similarly don't want to loom too large in my children's considerations. For example, I don't want them to choose the career or marriage partner that I would choose ... my "will" is that they make those choices themselves. I want them to be their own people, to develop their own personalities, to live their own stories ... not to huddle in my shadow. True, I don't want to be ignored either, but my desire to see them develop into unique people forces me to restrain myself, to not always give my opinion, to not step in and help every time they might ask for help, to not "do their homework for them," but rather to help them develop by not helping them sometimes.

Similarly, if God's goal in the universe is for us to develop — for us to make unpressured choices, to become who we will be not because "the Big Guy's looking" but for other more natural, unforced reasons (like courage, love, integrity, or justice) ... then perhaps God is forced to stay "subtle," behind-the-scenes, present but not too obvious, involved but also ignorable, here but hidden. C. S. Lewis said it like this in *The Screwtape Letters*: "He wants them to learn to walk and must therefore take away his hand."

Maybe God's very silence is actually intended to tell us something ... revealing a God who listens and thus pays us the unmatchable compliment of attention, a God who wants to make room for us to live our lives without constant intrusion, interference, or domination, a God who wants us to have a life, and not just be trivial accessories to God's own life. It's worth thinking about.

Why Aren't We Less Oblivious?

At the same time, God's apparent hiddenness could be a problem of ours. Perhaps many of us aren't looking for God; we are looking instead for our own interests, our next date, our next deal, our next purchase. Further than that, some of us may wish God not to exist ... since God's existence would likely entail moral limits and social responsibilities that we are eager to avoid. We may actually be suppressing evidence in order to maintain our illusion that we are not accountable to anyone. Or some of us might be so overcome by our troubles and worries that God could be putting signs of his existence all around us, and we would be oblivious.

Meanwhile, some of us are searching for God, and still God seems resistant to showing up sometimes. I know I have felt this way. The little faith I have has at times been stretched so thin ... I have waited so long ... searched for some sign of God's existence and presence and concern, but found nothing for so long ... God seemed to me to be taking very big risks with my endurance and character: more than once I have been on the verge of giving up on God altogether. God has seemed to me at times like a coach who pushed me so hard during practice that I almost quit the sport entirely.

Even here, though ... if faith and endurance are virtues, perhaps God has reasons to test us. A tested faith would surely prove more valuable than an untested one. Perhaps exercising endurance makes faith stronger, just as it does with muscles or concentration or commitments to friends and family. Perhaps the only growing, strengthening muscles are stretched and tired ones.

Having said all this, maybe we are ready to continue with our quest. No, nobody's asking you to think of God as an old man with a white beard. All we're saying in our pursuit of the monotheist path is that there is one God behind the universe, and this God must be amazing to have created all that exists—amazing, and relational—and thus worth "knowing" or experiencing.

Your Response

1. I believe God is impersonal/personal, because …
2. I believe God is relational/nonrelational, because …
3. This is how I will deal with issues of gender-inclusive language in reference to God:
4. This is how I respond to the question, "Why isn't God more obvious?"

Prayer

I do not wish to limit my thinking of you, but I am aware of my own limitations—constrained as I am by language, human thought patterns, my own experience and education, and the like. I feel that I am looking at an infinite sky through one small window. Yet rather than disparaging this limited viewpoint that I have as a disadvantage, I can be grateful for it: at least I am not staring at a windowless wall with no capacity to relate to you at all. This window—this set of experiences and starting points that are unique to me—is what I have been given, and so I continue in my search for you as you are, simply being myself, as I am. Please meet me where I am, and I will try to remain teachable and humble, open-minded and open-hearted, so that you can reveal more of yourself and your truth to me.

Don't **All** Paths Lead to **the** Same God?

This chapter is one of the more difficult chapters in the book. It addresses the issue of pluralism — how we deal with the multiplicity of religions.

Who Should Read This Chapter?

If you are familiar with or curious about the terms pluralism, postmodernism, and relativism, or if you have ever asked the question, "Don't all paths lead to the same God?" you shouldn't miss this chapter.

What Questions Does It Address?

If all religions are inspired, why do they contradict one another? How can one talk about which religions are right/wrong, better/worse, more/less helpful, and so on, without sounding elitist or judgmental? Is it possible that all religions possess some value even if they are not all equally true? How can one hold to a religion in a way that does not make him or her exclusive, elitist, or judgmental?

The diagram on the following page will be used to illustrate the relationship between various religions (the smaller circles) and the truth (the big circle, A).

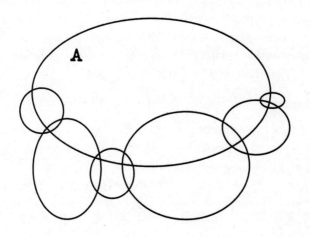

Don't **All** Paths Lead to **the** Same God?

This chapter is a test. It is a test of your ability to think clearly and keep your balance in an emotionally charged situation. It is a test of your objectivity. It may even be a test of your faith. If there is any part of this book that many people will not "like," my guess is that it will be this chapter. For that very reason, it is pretty important, and I saved it for last.

A New Situation

At the beginning of the twenty-first century, the search for faith is in one way different from the search at any other time in history. Imagine a young Philistine woman about three thousand years ago. Her search for faith was in many ways easier than ours. (Actually, she may not have had to search for it at all.) She had just one option: to be a Philistine. Sure, she was aware of many other nations—the Jews, the Hittites, the Amalekites, the Hivites. She was aware that they had other gods and religions. She knew that her religion was not the only religion in the world. But all the other nations were enemies of the Philistines, and so their gods were enemy gods—not an appealing option to her, since worshiping an enemy's god would be a betrayal of her own people!

Further, in those polytheistic times, people believed that gods were parochial, territorial. One god might be the right god for this geographical region, another for that. Choosing "the right god" was as simple as knowing where you were. When in Philistia . . .

Our hypothetical Philistine had another advantage: she didn't have much history behind her. The history of her religion consisted of the stories told by her mother and grandmother. There was little or no record of the scandals of her religious hierarchy centuries ago, or of its negative effects on the socioeconomic order in the previous century, or of its harmful psychological effects on the development of children over the years. Her faith could present itself as something pure, even perfect—an impossibility for us these days.

Furthermore, there was little or no science three thousand years ago. Claims made by her religion went pretty well undisputed. There was certainly no respected scientific establishment with a built-in skepticism for supernatural claims, constantly posing challenges to the claims of her religion.

Finally, all her associates shared her belief. She didn't buy milk from the local convenience store owned by the member of one religion, study chemistry from a professor of another, jog after work with three members of three different religions, and come home to a spouse of yet another. Her entire social milieu reinforced her unique faith . . . that "we" are "right." That "our" truth is the only true version for us.

The context in which our Philistine's faith flourished could not be more different from the context in which you and I seek faith today. In many, many ways, our Philistine's religious identification seemed natural—she didn't "choose" to worship the Philistine deity any more than she chose to speak the Philistine language.

Our young Philistine friend didn't have the "trilemma" faced by nearly every spiritual seeker today:

1. Some forces pull him to a particular commitment to a particular faith.
2. Some forces pull him to an equal tolerance for all faiths.
3. Some forces pull him away from any faith commitment at all.

Can you identify with this trilemma?

The Middle Element

If you are like many people these days, it is the middle element of that trilemma that is most troubling. Don't all paths lead to the same God? Why choose one faith over another? Isn't one a fool to narrow his options, when there are so many options to consider? Why not develop a tolerant, "accept-everything" faith, filled with the desired elements from each "aisle" in the religious market, like a grocery cart at the grocery store — a little bit of Hinduism, a few items from Christianity or Islam, some good Jewish and Buddhist products thrown in? Isn't it intolerant to claim that one religion is true, or truer than the others? Doesn't that imply an insult to all others? Doesn't it show unpardonable intolerance?

It almost makes you wish you were an ancient Philistine. From another vantage point, though, the advantages of our imaginary Philistine woman are themselves imaginary. If the goal is to find a faith that is relatively easy to accept and hard to doubt, then she had advantages indeed. But if the goal is to find a faith that is true — tested, considered, chosen, wanted, good—then you will probably agree our situation is preferable, in spite of the middle element, which we will call pluralism. So let's face pluralism head on.

Problems with Pluralism

"Pluralism" has several meanings, but for our purposes, pluralism means living with equal tolerance and respect for all belief systems. It means mirroring in our private lives the "religious freedom" laws of constitutional democracies—affording no preferences to any one religion. Sounds good, right? It means believing that all religions are equally true; that it doesn't matter which one you follow, as long as you're sincere. There is, inarguably, something appealing about pluralist spirituality. You might be surprised to hear my concerns about applying pluralism to one's personal spiritual search. I can explain my concerns with this "formula": If all religions are equally true....

... Then God Lies or Else Is Confused

If God told Mohammed that everyone must make a pilgrimage to Mecca, and God also told Jesus that it doesn't matter where you worship God, God speaks with forked tongue. If God told the followers of Moses that while it is morally wrong to eat ham, beef and chicken are okay ... but meanwhile God told the Hindus that eating any meat at all is immoral, what's God's problem—a poor memory? If God tells some people that men should dominate women, not allowing women to vote or drive or be seen in public with any skin exposed, while God tells other people that men and women are equal partners in the gift of life ... or if God tells some tribes and races they can be slaveholders, while telling others (perhaps the slaves themselves?) that all people have equal dignity ... I'm sorry, but God just lost me.

... Then God Prefers Some Religions over Others

If God tells one group of people that they should turn the other cheek when they are attacked, and then a few hundred years later tells some other people that they have the right to "convert with the sword" (i.e., "believe my religion or die"), I can't help but feel that God gave the second group an unfair advantage.

... Then All Religions Lie

Each religion claims that its approach is not just *an* option ... each religion claims to be *the* option, or at least the best option, or a better option than some others. But if all religions are in truth equally valid, then each religion that claims superiority (which is, in fact, every religion) is lying.

... Then Only One Belief Is Really True: Pluralism

If all belief systems claiming any superiority over their competitors are patent liars, then only one belief system is true: the belief system of pluralism, since it is the only one telling the truth that all belief systems are really equally valid.

... Then Pluralism Is True, But Pluralism Is Also False, Which Is Illogical

Follow me here. If all religions are equally true, as pluralism claims, then each religion is false when it claims that some or all other religions are not true ... which proves that pluralism (which claims that all religions are equally true) is false when it claims that all religions are true. Does that make sense? It shouldn't!

An Open Mind

Now having slammed pluralism (as we have defined it here) in this way, I hope you don't think I am for religious bigotry, holy wars, inquisitions, and the like. The fact is, I love living in a pluralistic society — a society of many races, religions, cultures, languages. How boring a monochrome society would be, after enjoying a full-color one. What's more, I share pluralism's disdain for any form of religious oppression, discrimination, or bigotry. I applaud every attempt for peace done in pluralism's name, since peacemaking is, to me, a truly spiritual work of faith. Pluralism is a big step up from bigotry, which in part explains its current popularity. But in the end, I think pluralism (as we have defined it here) is a miss, a near miss in some ways, but a miss nonetheless, not only for logical reasons (as we have seen) but also for practical reasons.

Practically speaking, different religions do agree on many things and they are allies on many fronts, but they disagree on many things too (as we saw in earlier chapters). They lay out very different paths to very different god-concepts and very different concepts of what life is all about. Your choice in religious commitment will determine a great deal about your life and future; you will live a very different kind of life depending on which path you follow. And globally, the world will turn into a very different place, depending on which religions predominate in our world. Some choices could be suicidal, some nightmarish, some hopeful, some ideal. (I hope you will pause and reread the previous two sentences.) Remember, bad religion can do some pretty horrific things. Not all religion is benign. You have probably heard the saying that one of the reasons we need good religion so much is that the alternative is not no religion, it's bad religion. So, how do we proceed in our search?

Four Guiding Principles

I have four guiding principles that have helped me face our modern faith trilemma.

1. Honor the Truth Wherever It Is Found

Many years ago, I committed myself to the Christian faith (more on that can be found in *Finding Faith—A Search for What Is Real*). As a Christian, I am taught to seek the truth, wisdom, and humility. That means that if a Buddhist teaches me, I gratefully honor the truth—because truth is truth, whoever brings it. Not only that, I should gratefully honor the bearer of that truth as well. The Bible is full of people of other faiths being used as messengers or conveyers of important truths. As a young Christian, I was too proud to admit that a Muslim could teach me, or that a Hindu could teach me, or that an atheist could teach me, but I have grown to learn to honor the truth wherever it is found. Doing so, I believe, doesn't make me less mature as a Christian, but rather more.

2. Honor the Glory Wherever It Is Found

Some matters are not matters of truth; they are matters of goodness or beauty, which I will refer to here together as "glory." When a Muslim mother cares for her children, works long hours, sacrifices, gives her all for their well-being, I see the glory of God in her as much as if she were a Jew, a Christian, my own mother. When an artist paints a beautiful painting, when a dancer moves with grace and wonder, when an architect lifts my spirits with light and space and texture and line, when a musician plays with heart and skill, when a teacher helps my child understand negative numbers, I don't need to ask whether she is an atheist, a Zoroastrian, or a Buddhist nun. The glory deserves to be honored wherever it is found, because it is ultimately a reflection of God's glory. Who else's could it be?

3. Honor People Especially When You Disagree

For me, as a Christian, I am commanded to love everyone — everyone. Everyone. Those with whom I agree are, in a sense, the easiest to love. But even the most faithless people love those who agree with them, so loving my colleagues is hardly an expression of faith: it's just an expression of common decency. My faith is proven by my ability to love with understanding and honor without bias those who are most different from me. I may not honor what they say or do. If they are spreading hatred, if they are stirring up fear or racism or greed, naturally, I will oppose their words and deeds. But I will try to honor them as people.

This bears a bit of elaboration. Have you noticed that relatively few people really aim to be evil, and that those who are evil often show up in surprising places — including "our" churches … and our shoes? Sometimes, those with whom we disagree prove themselves more honorable than we are. I remember one night I was leading a discussion group. We were talking about a passage of the Bible, and this one fellow, a visitor, was very talkative. By his third or fourth comment, I realized from his terminology that he was a member of a certain cult group notorious for mind control and other unsavory practices. I felt alarmed. He obviously was trying to infiltrate our group and cause division and attract converts to his group.

After the meeting, I cornered him. I was literally shaking with emotion. "I know where you're coming from, and your ideas aren't welcome around here ..." I let him have it with both barrels. After a moment of stunned silence, he replied, meekly, quietly, "Wow, I'm sorry. I just joined that group a few weeks ago. I had no idea that they were off the track. I've just blindly accepted everything they taught me. Thanks for telling me. I will have to rethink everything they said." His humility, his teachability, his vulnerability made me feel ashamed for assuming the worst about him. Ironically, even though so much of what he said that night was weird and warped, and even though I still think the group he had gotten involved with is a destructive, spiritually toxic group, that night he demonstrated more humility than I did. I learned something about good faith from this very fellow whom I was so intent on straightening out. Just when we think we can write off the evil guy "over there," we find evil pretty close to home.

4. It Is Okay to Not Know

Consider this. I don't know where my wife is at this moment. I don't know what she's thinking. I don't understand everything about her, even though we have been married for over twenty-five years. Just as I have some secrets she has never learned, I am sure she has some facets unknown to me. Should I be anxious about this lack of knowledge?

No. It's okay, because I have enough knowledge of her to love her, to trust her, to build a life with her. The same is true with God. There is so much about God I haven't even begun to understand, but the little I do understand is enough for me to love, trust, and build a life with God.

Among these unknowns for me—how God will treat people of other religions, how things will be after this life for people who don't believe but who lived better lives than many who do, exactly how God balances our free will with a degree of divine control over the universe, how God plans to redress the injustices of this world of ours, whether God has created life on other planets, how the universe was created, and so on, and so on. If I know enough to do justice, to be kind to others, to maintain a humble relationship with God, I don't need to know these other things ... or quarrel with those who have their own differing opinions.

Practicality Knocks

In sum, then, I believe the peacemaking attitude of pluralism is commendable, but as a friend of mine says, "An open mind is like an open window ... you need a screen to keep the bugs out." If we honor the truth wherever it is found and honor the glory wherever it is found, if we honor people especially when we disagree and can accept the fact that it's okay to not have all the answers, then the window is open. But how do we get the right screen? What standard do we use to reject some ideas as false and dangerous, and admit others as true and healthy?

If we were abstracted minds floating in ethereal zones of timelessness, perhaps we could have the luxury of debating this screening question for a few billion years. But we aren't. We are real people, with bills to pay and diapers to change and grades to earn and contracts to fulfill and conflicts to resolve. Every day is a once-in-a-lifetime possibility. Every day lived is one less to live.

Every day we live by some faith, good or bad, strong or weak, growing or stagnant or deteriorating. We need some practical tools to help us sort through the messages of various religions. We need some screening tools.

Here are four screening tools I have applied in my search, with good effect.

1. Does the belief make sense? Does it possess internal intellectual integrity and coherence? Does it fit reality as I know it? As a system of belief, does it hold water? Is the belief merely comforting or pleasant or helpful, or is it more? Is it probable, convincing, believable?

2. Is the belief workable and livable? If everyone on earth held this belief, would the results be good? Does the belief lead to health and life and hope, or would it lead to self-destruction and despair?

3. Do I want to associate with the people who profess this belief? Does the quality of their community life authenticate or undermine their message? Does their belief produce good fruit in their lives as individuals and as a community? Here I don't expect perfection, but I do expect honesty, forgiveness, love, unselfishness, acceptance, vitality.

4. If I affiliated with this group, would I feel comfortable bringing an interested friend to visit? I expect a healthy faith to be contagious, so I expect that I will have friends who want to visit whatever faith community I am part of—if it is indeed nurturing a healthy faith in me. Would they, wherever they're coming from, be as welcome as I am there? Would I be ashamed to bring them there, knowing the experience there would be for them incomprehensible, unwelcoming, offensive, or irrelevant?

What about the Original Question?

Don't all religions lead to God? Well, I wouldn't put it past God to be able to get through to people in (or out of) any religion. In my experience, God is amazingly merciful, so I wouldn't be shocked at all if God's mercy extends to surprising lengths, in unexpected directions, to people you never would have guessed. If, like me, you take the story of Jesus seriously, you can't be too quick to claim to have everything figured out; he said the prostitutes sometimes had a better shot at entering the kingdom of God than the priests did!

But even so, please don't let that lead you to this unwise—I would even say tragic—conclusion: "It doesn't matter what you believe." The pluralists are right, I think, to have an aversion to the concept of a narrow, exclusive god who enjoys fueling petty religious squabbles. But God would be right, I think, to expect people equipped with state-of-the-art brains to care about the truth, to use their minds, to do their best to face reality and respond to it. An "I don't care—whatever" attitude toward the choice of one's path through life hardly seems the right choice, don't you agree? Do you remember what we said in this regard about good faith ... that the best way, perhaps, to a right faith (i.e. a faith in line with the truth) would be via developing a good faith, since a good faith will, by definition, be humble enough to admit it is wrong and self-correct, and active enough to keep pursuing truth and learning, thus leading over time to an increasingly accurate, truth-reflecting faith?

As we considered in chapter 2, it is uncertain how much certainty we humans can attain, but it is pretty clear that we ought to aspire to all the truth we can. How much truth we can grasp, and how firmly we can grasp it, is unclear; it is clear that we should always be reaching, reaching, reaching.

So it matters which path you choose, and it matters how you pursue your chosen path. All paths aren't all the same. Although all will no doubt yield some truth, they can't all be equally true, and so it's no use living in denial about the necessity of making choices, sometimes hard choices. In these pluralistic times, we have more live options than ever before—which presents us with opportunity and responsibility. We will need both open windows and good screens.

The following diagram has helped me to respond to this question, "Don't all paths lead to the same God?"

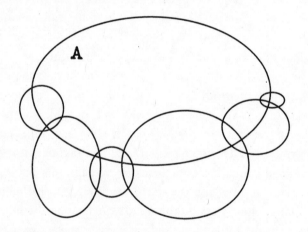

Imagine that circle A represents the ultimately true religion, possessing all truth (and no falsehood) about God, life, the universe. If anybody claims to "have" this religion—in other words, if anybody claims to have captured the whole truth perfectly in his or her own mind—we might be justified in laughing in his or her face. Whether he or she is proud or naive, either way, the laugh would probably be therapeutic.

Let the other five smaller circles represent various religions. One could be Buddhism, one Christianity, another Hinduism, and so forth. Or for that matter, each could be individual versions of one religion — the belief systems of five members from my church, or five Jewish rabbis, for example. (After all, no two of us has exactly the same religion.) As we would expect, each circle "covers" some truth, but not all, and each includes some misconceptions, misunderstandings, falsehood, and so forth. There is some overlap among them, but there are significant differences too. Clearly, each circle has something to teach and something to learn from all the others. In this light, instead of saying each religion is equally valid, we would be wiser to say that each religion has real value, conveying a viewpoint that can challenge and enrich the others and be challenged and enriched by the others.

Still, no circle comprehends or contains all the truth, meaning that no human mind or system sees it all and grasps it all. If this is the case — and it is hard for me to imagine any other scenario — then the essence of what we have called "good faith" becomes clear: to have good faith, I must see that there is a difference between having faith in my circle and having faith in the Big Circle, which is, admittedly, beyond me.

In other words, there is a very significant difference between having faith in my religion (i.e., my circle, my belief system, my current understanding) and faith in God's religion (i.e., God's truth, the truth as God sees it and knows it). Good faith has no choice but to be a circle, to define itself in some way, but it must do so with humility, tentativeness, openness to correction, even more, a curiosity and hunger for instruction and growth and learning. (Very likely, this is what Jesus was referring to when he spoke of our need to have the faith of a child.) It must not take itself too seriously. It must remain open to ongoing expansion, adjustment, and movement, so that it will become more and more "in sync" with the big circle of truth.

But how does one realign and redraw his circle? How does one bring it more in sync with God's truth, whatever that might be? How does one gather more data so as to enrich, adjust, move, and improve one's circle of understanding? Those are the questions that we will focus on in the second volume, *Finding Faith—A Search for What Is Real*.

Your Response

1. I could/could not follow the critique of the pluralistic view that says, "All religions are equally true."
2. I affirm the following guiding principles for my spiritual search:

   Honor the truth wherever it is found.
   Honor the glory wherever it is found.
   It is okay to not know.

3. I affirm the following screening and affiliation tools from the chapter:
4. Here is my response to the "big circle" diagram:

Resources

C. S. Lewis's wonderful children's stories, *The Chronicles of Narnia*, have much to offer to a spiritual seeker. The final volume, *The Last Battle*, depicts an interchange between the great lion Aslan and the follower of a patently bad religion that takes an unexpected turn. I highly recommend the whole series.

Steve Martin's film *Leap of Faith* explores similar territory.

Prayer

God, far be it from me to judge people of other religions. I am not sure how you work in various religions, and how you evaluate each religion; that is beyond me, and I leave it to you. But I must evaluate the claims of the religious options open to me, and I must make choices. Please guide me in my choices, God. Don't let religion become a detour in my search for you, and in my desire to live in a way that pleases you. I don't want to trust in a religion instead of you, but rather, I want to trust in you and grow in my faith with the help of a religion, or better put, with your help through whatever religion is best for me. Again, please guide me, God. I don't want to lean on my own understanding.

Conclusion: Next Steps

Perhaps you feel as I do: that we have decided to go on a journey. We have come to the airport, chosen a destination, picked up our ticket, gotten through airport security, found our gate, boarded our flight, stowed our carry-on luggage, put on our seatbelt, and stored our tray tables in their upright and locked position. The captain has told the flight attendants to prepare for take-off and we are paused on the runway. The jet engines are beginning to roar.

We have come a long way, but we haven't gotten off the ground yet. The purpose of this book was simply to get us to this point. The next steps are up to you—or perhaps I should say they are up to you and God together. You could put this book down and say, "Well, that was interesting," and go on in life with little effect. Or your effort in reading and thinking through this book could mark a major milestone in your life. It could be the beginning of an ongoing, lifelong journey. If you are saying, "Okay! Let's take off!"—then here are some suggestions for your next steps. I haven't numbered them because I want you to prayerfully decide for yourself which steps to take and which order you would like to take them.

____ I would like to read this book again.

____ I would like to find some people to discuss this book with. Specifically, I'd like to ask . . .

____ I would like to continue the journey by reading the second volume, *Finding Faith—A Search for What Is Real.*

____ I would like to let the thoughts I've encountered in this book settle for a while in my mind and heart.

____ I would like to find a pastor, priest, rabbi, trusted friend, or other spiritual mentor to help me process my remaining questions. Here are some people I could ask for recommendations, or here is the person I would like to speak with …

____ I would like to find a faith community to join to help me take the next steps in my journey. Here are some people I could ask for recommendations about a good faith community …

____ I would like to do additional reading or research on one particular subject or theme from this book, specifically …

____ I would like to keep praying for guidance from God in my search. To help me pray, I would like to ____write my prayers in a journal, ____develop the habit of praying when I wake up and go to bed each day, ____pray before each meal, ____join a small group that prays.

____ I would like to conduct a "faith experiment." For the next thirty days, I would like to put my doubts and skepticism aside and seek to live as if God existed and I believed. I will "test drive" faith for thirty days, after which I will either continue my search, repeat the experiment, or discontinue it. For these thirty days, here is what I would like to do…

____ I would like to consult the author's website for more resources (www.anewkindofchristian.com).

At the end of each chapter I included a suggested prayer for you to pray. I would like to conclude this book with my own prayer for you.

God, over these many years I have come to believe in you as being kind, gracious, compassionate, forgiving, good, and faithful. I have experienced so many blessings, so many good things in my journey with you. Yet I know that this path of faith has often been difficult. I have faced so many questions, so many unknowns, so many disillusionments and struggles. I pray for this person, reading this book, at this moment. May this reader be sustained through the difficulties. May they somehow know that you are here, with them, now and forever. May they know that you care about them, and that you will faithfully guide them as they continue to seek faith, as they continue to seek you. When they are tempted to give up, please send them encouragement. When they get distracted, please get their attention again. When they need spiritual companionship, please send them the right person at the right time. When they need a faith community, help them find the one that is just right for them.

Please, God, use the words of this book to help every reader, but Lord, beyond these words, please somehow touch them in their hearts so they encounter you directly. The ancient prophet Jeremiah wrote, "They will seek me, and they will find me, when they seek with all their heart." Jesus said, "Seek first God's kingdom and God's justice, and all that you need will come to you." One of Jesus' early followers wrote, "God, who began the good work in you, will bring it to completion. . . ." Help each reader to believe these words as being true for them. Lord, they have taken their seat for a journey of faith. They are on the runway. Please be their pilot, and let them soar with you. Amen.

Sources and Resources

Behe, Michael. *Darwin's Black Box*. New York: Free Press, 1996.

Berry, Wendell. *Life Is a Miracle*. New York: Counterpoint, 2000.

Borg, Marcus. *The Heart of Christianity: Rediscovering a Life of Faith*. San Francisco: HarperSanFrancisco, 2003.

Card, Orson Scott. *The Memory of Earth*. Alvin Maker Series. New York: Tor Books, 1994.

_____. *Seventh Son*. Alvin Maker Series. New York: Tor Books, 1993.

Glynn, Patrick. *God: The Evidence*. Centerport, NY: Forum, 1997.

Haught, John. *God after Darwin: A Theology of Evolution*. New York: Westview, 2001.

Heeren, Fred. *Show Me God*. Wheeling, IL: Searchlight, 1995.

Kreeft, Peter. *Yes or No: Straight Answers to Tough Questions about Christianity*. San Francisco: Ignatius, 1991.

Küng, Hans. *Does God Exist? An Answer for Today*. 1980. Reprint, New York: Herder & Herder, 1994. 864 pages.

_____. *On Being a Christian*. 1974. Reprint, New York: Doubleday, 1984.

Lewis, C. S. *Mere Christianity*. 1943. Reprint, New York: HarperCollins, 2001.

_____. *Miracles: A Preliminary Study*. 1947. Reprint, New York: HarperCollins, 2001.

_____. *Surprised by Joy*. Reprint, New York: Harcourt, Brace, 1995.

McDowell, Josh. *Answers to Tough Questions Skeptics Ask about the Christian Faith*. Carol Stream, IL: Tyndale, 1986.

_____. *Evidence That Demands a Verdict*. San Bernardino, CA: Here's Life Publishers, 1972.

McLaren, Brian D. *The Church on the Other Side*. Revised edition. Grand Rapids: Zondervan, 2006.

Newbigin, Lesslie. *The Gospel in a Pluralist Society*. Grand Rapids: Eerdmans, 1989.

_____. *The Open Secret*. Revised edition. Grand Rapids: Eerdmans, 1995.

Percy, Walker. "The Message in the Bottle." In *The Message in the Bottle*. New York: Farrar, Straus & Giroux, 1975.

_____. *Lancelot*. 1977. Reprint, New York: Picador, 1999.

_____. *The Last Gentleman*. 1966. Reprint, New York: Picador, 1999.

_____. *The Second Coming*. New York: Farrar, Straus & Giroux, 1980.

Polkinghorne, John. *The Faith of a Physicist*. Minneapolis: Fortress Press, 1996.

Ross, Hugh. *Creation and Time*. Colorado Springs: NavPress, 1994.

Smith, Huston. *The World's Religions*. San Francisco: HarperSanFrancisco, 1991.

Strobel, Lee. *The Case for Faith*. Grand Rapids: Zondervan, 2000.

Tolstoy, Leo. *A Confession*. 1879–81. Translated by David Patterson. New York: Norton, 1983.

Wright, N. T. *Simply Christian*. Grand Rapids/San Francisco: Zondervan/HarperSanFrancisco, 2006.

Yancey, Philip. *What's So Amazing About Grace?* Grand Rapids: Zondervan, 1997.

We want to hear from you. Please send your comments about this book to us in care of zreview@zondervan.com. Thank you.

ZONDERVAN.com/
AUTHORTRACKER
follow your favorite authors